Dandelion

Phonics Instructional Manual

Kindergarten

PhonicBooks®

DK Learning

Produced for DK by Westchester Education Services

Publisher Sarah Forbes
Managing Editor Katherine Neep
Managing Art Editor Sarah Corcoran
Senior Editor Amelia Jones
Production Controller Isabell Schart
Production Editor Shanker Prasad

First American Edition, 2024
Published in the United States by DK Publishing,
a division of Penguin Random House LLC
1745 Broadway, 20th Floor, New York, NY 10019

24 25 26 27 28 10 9 8 7 6 5 4 3 2 1
001-344993-Oct/2024

Published in Great Britain by
Phonic Books, an imprint of Dorling Kindersley Limited

A catalog record for this book
is available from the Library of Congress.
ISBN 978-0-5938-4852-4

Printed and bound in China

CONTENTS

INTRODUCTION

WHAT IS PHONIC BOOKS?

Phonic Books specializes in publishing systematic synthetic phonic books for beginner and catch-up readers.

The company was founded in 2006 by Wendy Tweedie, Tami Reis-Frankfort, and Clair Wilson, three special needs teachers passionate about teaching all children to read. Using their expertise, they set about developing phonic reading books for young children and older readers.

Following demand from customers, the range has extended from the initial 10 titles to over 300 today, and is continuing to grow. Our US range of books caters for students in Pre-K and Kindergarten to older readers in Middle School.

With a growing reputation for quality and effectiveness, our books are now used by schools, tutors, and parents in the US and 40 countries around the world.

HOW TO USE THIS MANUAL ?

The Phonics Instructional Manual Kindergarten is organized into three main parts. The first part introduces foundational concepts and prevalent teaching strategies in phonics instruction.

In the second part, the focus shifts to the practical elements of the Phonic Books program for Kindergarten. It provides an overview of the program, complementary teaching methods, a scheme of work, guidelines for lesson planning, and strategies for assessment, providing teachers with the necessary tools for effective teaching.

The third part is the heart of the manual: the lesson plans for the Phonic Books program for Kindergarten. The initial set of lesson plans align with the Dandelion Launchers series, a set of stories (readers) designed for beginners which is organized into 20 progressive stages. The lesson plans for Kindergarten align with the first 15 stages and require the use of both the Dandelion Launchers readers and the corresponding activity books. The readers act as the instructional text, introducing new letters and sounds, while the activity books provide supplementary exercises in reading, writing, spelling, and comprehension.

Each stage in the Dandelion Launchers series is designed to build a gradual understanding of phonics, introducing new letters and sounds while reinforcing previously learned phonics and high-frequency words. It begins with sounds of the alphabet in Stages 1–7 and progresses to consonant blends and digraphs in Stages 8–15.

The final set of lesson plans extends to more advanced spelling patterns: VCe or silent 'e' spellings in the Dandelion Readers VCe Spellings set.

The lesson plans are adaptable and can be integrated with different US phonics curricula. Teachers can access curriculum mapping grids on the Phonic Books website to align these lesson plans with their specific curriculum requirements.

A glossary of terms is provided at the back of the book.

ADVICE FOR TEACHERS

Decodable books, such as the Phonic Books series, are important for teaching foundational skills. These controlled texts allow the student to practice their phonetic knowledge and read successfully at each developmental stage. They also encourage students to use the most effective and reliable reading strategies for life (sounding out words).

Many teachers find they need additional resources to support students who are beginner and older readers. For example: students may face challenges with letter sounds, phonemic awareness, retaining phonics lessons, or have gaps in their vocabulary. The Phonic Books series, encompassing both decodable readers and activity books, can be used as a classroom resource in various ways: with a whole class, in reading groups, or in 1:1 reading support.

The Phonic Books website also contains many free teaching resources as well as advice for teachers. The resources include phonics infographics, teaching strategies, word lists, word chains, dictation exercises, phonic code tables, high-frequency word charts, game templates, and progress trackers. The website also includes assessment tools such as reading assessments and assessment cards, alongside advice on how to use the Phonic Books series in different educational settings.

SUPPLEMENTARY RESOURCES

This instructional manual primarily focuses on the Dandelion Launchers series of decodable books and the corresponding activity books. However, Phonic Books has a wealth of parallel books and supplementary materials to help teachers with their phonics instruction. More details are provided in the program overview section on page 19.

FOUNDATIONS OF PHONICS

WHAT IS PHONICS?

Phonics is a method of teaching reading and writing that focuses on the relationship between sounds (**phonemes**) and their spellings (**graphemes**). It involves teaching students to connect sounds in words with letters or groups of letters and to blend these sounds to form recognizable words.

English has a complex writing system. It has 26 letters but roughly 44 sounds (this depends on pronunciation), leading to roughly 160+ different spellings for these 44 sounds. In order to teach them in a methodical way, they have been organized according to the 44 sounds they spell. This organization is called the **Alphabetic Code** or **Phonic Code**. Research has shown that students who are taught these sound–letter correspondences will learn to decode words more successfully. Decoding underpins fluency, and fluency underpins reading comprehension.

Unlike languages with "transparent" writing systems like Italian and Spanish, where letters spell sounds in a simple and consistent way, English has an "opaque" writing system. Its complexity is a result of layers of adopted words from different languages and shifts in pronunciation over many years. Consequently, learning to read in English is more time-consuming, often taking years compared to the few months it might take in more phonetically consistent languages.

Where to start in phonics instruction

All phonics programs start with the sounds of the letters of the alphabet. The Phonic Books program starts with the simple principle of one letter corresponding to one sound. Students initially learn a few letters at a time, building simple words as they progress.

THE ALPHABETIC CODE abc

The **Alphabetic Code** is the framework that shows how the 44 sounds of English are represented by letters and letter combinations.

Key aspects include:

1. 26 letters are used and reused in many different combinations to represent the 44 sounds of speech.
2. A sound can be represented by 1–4 letters.
3. A sound can be spelled in numerous ways.
4. A spelling (or grapheme) can represent different sounds.

Students need to recognize these letter–sound relationships automatically to become fluent readers. Due to the complexity of the code, many phonics programs will first introduce a simple part of it and later the more complex letter–sound correspondences.

CHALLENGES IN THE ALPHABETIC CODE

Navigating the complexities of the Alphabetic Code can be a daunting task, especially for students learning English. The Alphabetic Code is marked by a notable disparity between the sounds (phonemes) and the letters (graphemes) used to represent them. This mismatch leads to various challenges.

English uses the same letters to represent different sounds because of the mismatch between the number of letters and sounds. Because of this disparity, letters are reused to spell the extra sounds. For example, the letters 's' and 'h' together spell a completely new sound: /sh/ as in the word "**sh**ip." This is a **consonant digraph**. That wouldn't be such a problem if our Alphabetic Code were simple and straightforward—but it isn't!

Sounds spelled by 1–4 letters

Sounds in English can be spelled by 1–4 letters. In the word "cat," each letter spells one sound. In the word "chip," the consonant digraph 'ch' spells the sound /ch/. Here two letters spell one sound. In the word "night," the vowel team 'igh' spells one sound /ie/. Finally, in the word "dough," the four-letter spelling 'ough' spells just one sound, /oe/.

Multiple spellings for one sound

A further complication is that a sound can be spelled in different ways. For example, the sound /ae/ can be spelled in numerous ways: r**ai**n, m**ay**, c**a**m**e**, th**ey**, w**eigh**, v**ei**l, gr**ea**t, etc. Students need to learn these alternatives so that when they see them within words, they know how to sound them out. And when they learn to encode (spell), students will need to remember which alternative fits in which word. Multiple spellings for one sound are not covered in this manual.

One spelling, multiple sounds

Not only are there different ways to spell these sounds, but once learned, students find that some spellings can be pronounced in different ways. For example, the spelling 'ea' spells the sound /e/ in "h**ea**d," /ee/ in "m**ea**t," and /ae/ in "gr**ea**t."

These are difficult concepts to teach, and students need a structured system to learn them. This is why it is so important that reading instruction is taught in a systematic and structured way. When taught well, the Alphabetic Code is unlocked and students learn to decode and encode any word.

UNLOCKING THE ALPHABETIC CODE

Demonstrating the mechanics

We begin by illustrating the basic mechanics of the English language: reading from left to right, and understanding how individual letters and their combinations represent distinct sounds in speech.

Teaching the code

We then teach the Alphabetic Code, focusing on specific letter–sound correspondences in the English language.

Neglecting to teach the Alphabetic Code risks depriving students of the key to learning to read and the vast opportunities for learning and exploration it offers.

THE ALPHABETIC CODE

Consonant sound spellings

/j/

j **j**et
g **g**entle
ge bar**ge**
dge ju**dge**

/n/

n **n**o
nn pla**nn**ing
kn **kn**ow
gn **gn**at
pn **pn**eumonia

/z/

z **z**ip
zz bu**zz**
s i**s**
se choo**se**
ze snoo**ze**
x **x**ylophone

/r/

r **r**at
wr **wr**ite
rr ca**rr**y
rh **rh**ino

/h/

h **h**ot
wh **wh**ole

/qu/ (/k/ + /w/)

qu **qu**een

/t/

t **t**in
tt ge**tt**ing
ed jump**ed**
bt de**bt**
pt **pt**erodactyl
te grani**te**

/x/ (/k/ + /s/)

x fo**x**
cc a**cc**ept

/y/

y **y**es

/ng/

ng si**ng**
n pi**n**k

/s/

s **s**ip
ss gra**ss**
se hou**se**
c **c**ent
ce voi**ce**
st ca**st**le

/v/

v **v**ery
ve ha**ve**

/ch/

ch **ch**ip
tch ma**tch**

/b/

b **b**ig
bb ra**bb**it

/th/ (voiced)

th **th**at

/th/ (unvoiced)

th **th**in

/f/

f **f**at
ff sta**ff**
ph **ph**one
gh lau**gh**
ffe gira**ffe**

/w/

w **w**ig
wh **wh**en

/g/

g ra**g**
gg ju**gg**le
gh **gh**ost
gu **gu**est

/d/

d **d**id
ed grabb**ed**
dd mu**dd**le

/l/

l **l**ip
ll fu**ll**
le app**le**
el trav**el**
il pup**il**
al fin**al**

/sh/

sh **sh**op
ch ma**ch**ine
s **s**ugar

/p/

p ho**p**
pp ha**pp**y

/m/

m **m**an
mm su**mm**er
mb la**mb**
mn Autu**mn**

/k/

k **k**ite
c **c**at
ck du**ck**
ch **ch**ord

/zh/

s lei**s**ure
ge presti**ge**
z sei**z**ure

THE ALPHABETIC CODE

Vowel sound spellings

/oe/	
o	m**o**st
o–e	n**o**t**e**
oe	t**oe**
oa	b**oa**t
ow	gr**ow**
ough	th**ough**
ou	s**ou**l
ew	s**ew**

/i/	
i	**i**n
y	m**y**th

/o/	
o	n**o**t
a	w**a**s

/ie/	
i	w**i**ld
ie	p**ie**
i–e	l**i**k**e**
igh	n**igh**t
y	dr**y**
eigh	h**eigh**t

/ee/	
e	m**e**
ee	m**ee**t
ea	s**ea**t
e–e	**e**v**e**
ie	ch**ie**f
y	funn**y**
ey	k**ey**
ei	rec**ei**ve
i	var**i**ation
eo	p**eo**ple

/ae/	
a	t**a**ble
ai	r**ai**n
a–e	g**a**m**e**
ea	gr**ea**t
ay	s**ay**
ey	th**ey**
ei	v**ei**n
aigh	str**aigh**t
eigh	**eigh**t

/or/	
or	f**or**
our	y**our**
ore	m**ore**
oor	d**oor**
oar	b**oar**d
ar	w**ar**m

‘aw’	
aw	l**aw**n
awe	**awe**some
a	b**a**ll
al	w**al**k
au	**Au**gust
ough	f**ough**t
augh	d**augh**ter

/e/	
e	b**e**d
ea	br**ea**d
ai	s**ai**d
ie	fr**ie**nd
eo	l**eo**pard

/er/	
er	p**er**k
ur	t**ur**n
ir	g**ir**l
or	w**or**ld
ear	l**ear**n
ar	coll**ar**
yr	zeph**yr**

/oo/	
oo	c**oo**k
oul	c**oul**d
u	p**u**t
o	w**o**man

/a/	
a	c**a**t

/ear/	
ear	n**ear**
eer	d**eer**
ere	h**ere**

/u/	
u	t**u**b
ou	t**ou**ch
o–e	s**o**m**e**
a	**a**bout
o	M**o**nday
oo	bl**oo**d

/ar/	
ar	c**ar**

/ow/	
ow	c**ow**
ou	**ou**t
ough	dr**ough**t

/oi/	
oi	j**oi**n
oy	b**oy**

/ue/	
u–e	m**u**l**e**
u	p**u**pil
ew	f**ew**
ue	c**ue**

/air/	
air	ch**air**
are	d**are**
ear	b**ear**
eir	th**eir**
ere	wh**ere**
ayor	m**ayor**
ayer	pr**ayer**
ae	**ae**rosol

/oo/	
oo	b**oo**t
ue	bl**ue**
ew	gr**ew**
u	s**u**per
ui	s**ui**t
u–e	fl**u**t**e**
ou	s**ou**p
oe	sh**oe**
o	d**o**
ough	thr**ough**

PHONICS CONCEPTS

What is a phoneme?

A **phoneme** is the smallest unit of sound in a word. For example: the word "cat" has three phonemes: /k /a/ /t/.

Why do we need phonemes?

Phonemes are essential in learning to read and write because they are the building blocks of words, enabling us to segment and blend sounds to form words. Understanding phonemes helps in the development of literacy skills.

The English Alphabetic Code is based on the 44 phonemes in the English language. The letters of the alphabet represent those sounds with 160+ letter combinations.

When we teach reading, we need to show how the Alphabetic Code works: that the *letters* on the page *spell sounds in words.*

What is a grapheme?

A **grapheme** is a written representation or *spelling* of a sound (phoneme) in a word. A grapheme can be spelled by 1–4 letters.

In a **1-letter grapheme**, each sound is spelled by one letter:

c → /k/ a → /a/ t → /t/

In a **2-letter grapheme**, a sound is spelled by two letters:

sh → /sh/ o → /o/ p → /p/

In a **3-letter grapheme**, a sound is spelled by three letters:

n → /n/ igh → /ie/ t → /t/

In a **4-letter grapheme**, a sound is spelled by four letters:

d → /d/ ough → /oe/

What is a digraph?

A **digraph** is when two letters represent one sound in a word (phoneme).

di → two (from Greek)

graph → to write letters (from Greek)

Therefore, a digraph means two written letters.

A **consonant digraph** is when two letters represent a consonant sound. For example: the letters 's' and 'h' spell the sound /sh/ in the word "ship."

A **vowel team** is when two or more letters represent a vowel sound. For example: the letters 'a' and 'i' spell the sound /ae/ in the word "rain."

What are consonant blends?

Consonant blends are also called **consonant clusters**. These are two or more adjacent consonants in a word that spell two separate sounds. For example, in the word "stop" the letters 's' and 't' spell the sounds /s/ and /t/.

stop

What are Vowel–Consonant–e (VCe) spellings?

A **Vowel–Consonant–e (VCe) spelling** is when the spelling for the vowel sounds /ae/, /ee/, /ie/, /oe/, and /ue/ is split by a consonant:

/ae/	a–e	→	gate
/ee/	e–e	→	eve
/ie/	i–e	→	fine
/oe/	o–e	→	hope
/ue/	u–e	→	cute

What is a schwa?

A schwa is a weak vowel sound in an unstressed syllable.

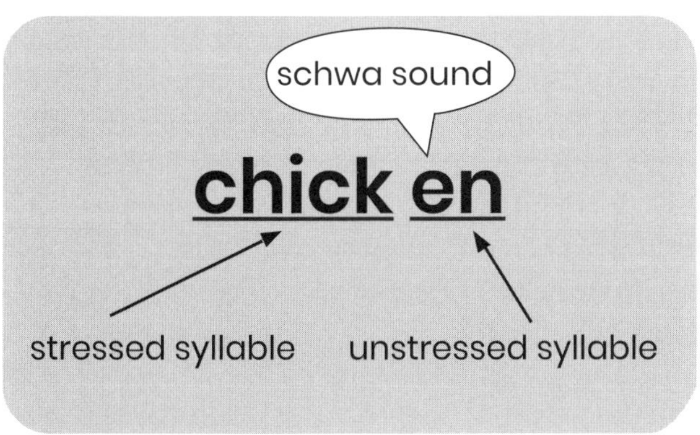

An example of a schwa is 'e' because it is a weak vowel sound in an unstressed syllable. It gets swallowed up when we pronounce the word "chicken," becoming "chickin" or "chick'n." We need to teach students to use their "spelling voice" in order to spell the word correctly and not as they hear it.

LANGUAGE UNITS AND PRINCIPLES

Words to morphemes

There are different ways of looking at a word.

A **word** is a distinct meaningful unit of speech or writing.

Letters are characters used for representing sounds in speech.

Syllables are mouthfuls of words.

Phonemes are speech sounds in words.

Graphemes are spellings of sounds in words.

Morphemes are units of meaning in words.

Distinguishing phonology, phonological awareness, and phonics

Phonology is an area of linguistics that deals with speech sound systems and sound patterns of spoken language.

Phonological awareness is the ability to break down words into smaller parts: syllables (mag net), alliteration (Bobby beetle bounced), onset and rime (m at), and phonemic awareness (m a t).

Phonemic awareness is the ability to identify and manipulate individual sounds in words (to blend, segment, and manipulate sounds).

Phonics is the teaching of:

- letter/sound correspondences for reading and spelling: c a t = /k/ /a/ /t/
- blending of individual letters/sounds for reading: m a t
- segmenting of individual sounds/letters for spelling: m a t

The Alphabetic Principle

The **Alphabetic Principle** is a fundamental concept in phonics instruction.

According to this principle, written letters or graphemes correspond to specific sounds (phonemes) of a spoken language. These sounds come together to form words.

This is crucial for learning to read, as it allows students to decode written text into spoken language.

Mapping words vs learning words by sight

There are two key word recognition strategies in reading: **mapping words** and **learning words by sight**.

Learning a word by shape (sight) is inefficient and clogs up precious memory.

house memorize one word by shape

Learning to map words helps readers to generalize and continue to "self-teach" new words.

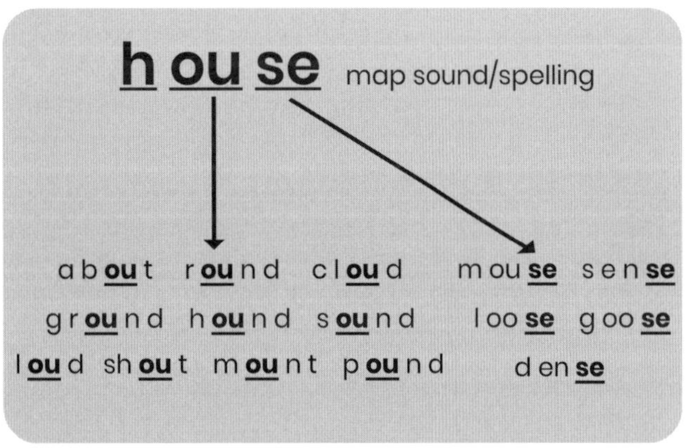

HIGH-FREQUENCY WORDS

High-frequency words are words that appear very frequently in stories and other written texts, such as "or" and "the." It is important for students to learn how to recognize these words quickly and effortlessly.

Many high-frequency words do not follow regular phonetic patterns or are not decodable until students have learned more advanced phonics patterns. This irregularity can make them challenging for students to decode them using phonics rules alone. Therefore, it is important for students to learn these words using different recognition strategies. In some other phonics programs, these words might be referred to as "tricky words," "sight words," or "heart words."

Teaching high-frequency words helps students read more smoothly and focus their decoding efforts on less common and more complex words. Mastery of high-frequency words significantly enhances reading fluency and comprehension, allowing students to become more confident readers.

High-frequency words: teaching by sound, not shape

Teaching high-frequency words by sound rather than shape offers a more effective approach to phonics instruction.

When learning high-frequency words through this method, students not only memorize these words more efficiently, but they also gain skills that are transferable to new, unfamiliar words.

This approach enhances the ability of students to decode and understand a wider range of vocabulary, supporting their overall reading fluency and comprehension.

How to teach students to spell high-frequency words

When we teach high-frequency words as whole words, we are encouraging students to remember them by shape. This method contradicts the phonics approach that explains that all words can be decoded—but some have complex spellings! Unfortunately, many of the common words beginner readers encounter are such words.

So how do we combine phonics with teaching difficult high-frequency words? Build on the knowledge the reader already has and explicitly teach the tricky part.

Here is an example of how to teach the word "car," which contains the phoneme /ar/ that is introduced in Dandelion Readers Level 1 Book 12 in the Phonic Books program.

1. Segment the word into its phonemes (sounds).

car

/c/ /ar/

2. Map the word showing its grapheme (spellings of the phonemes).

c ar

3. Identify the tricky spellings in the word and show familiar words with these spellings.

c ar

4. Ask the student to say the words as they write the word.

'c' 'ar' → car

DECODING AND ENCODING

It is important for teachers to distinguish between the concepts of **decoding** and **encoding**. Decoding involves translating symbols or letters into sounds and words.

Encoding, on the other hand, is the reverse process, where words and sounds are translated into symbols or letters.

For students to understand this reversible code, it's important that decoding and encoding are taught together. This approach helps students understand that "mat" can be segmented into the sounds /m/ /a/ /t/ and spelled out, just as these sounds can be blended together to form the word "mat." By teaching reading and spelling together in the same lesson, teachers can provide a more comprehensive and effective lesson.

The following figure overleaf illustrates how the two essential skills of decoding and encoding work in tandem to form a complete understanding of reading and spelling.

Decoding

(translating symbols/letters to sounds and words)

is the reverse of ⟷

Encoding

(translating words/sounds into symbols/letters)

For students to understand this reversible code, decoding and encoding should be taught together!

mat /m/ /a/ /t/ "mat" →

Sound out the words and blend them together into a word.

mat /m/ /a/ /t/ *"mat"* →

Sound out the words and blend them together into a word.

Teach reading and spelling in the same lesson!

SYNTHETIC PHONICS VS ANALYTIC PHONICS

In **synthetic phonics** instruction, the reader is taught to sound out individual sounds in a word and blend these sounds together to form the word. This method emphasizes the *synthesis* (blending) of individual sounds into a word. For example, the word "frog" is learned by sounding out each phoneme, /f/ /r/ /o/ /g/, and then blending these sounds to say "frog."

Conversely, **analytic phonics** focuses on teaching readers to break the word up into parts. This begins with an *analysis* of the whole word, which is broken into onset and rime, e.g. 'fr' + 'og' → "frog."

The conclusion based on research, notably Watson and Johnson (2004) and the Rose Report (2006), is that synthetic phonics is the most effective way to teach all children to read.

Analytic phonics often includes using known words as analogies. For example: if you know that "cat" ends with 'at' then you know that "mat" must also end with 'at.'

Systematic Synthetic Phonics

Systematic Synthetic Phonics (SSP) is a method that focuses on the systematic instruction of phonics. In this approach, students are taught to recognize graphemes and their corresponding phonemes. SSP involves a sequenced order of teaching where children first learn simple letter–sound correspondences (like 's' for /s/) and then progress to more complex sound patterns (like 'igh' for /ie/). The method emphasizes the blending or synthesizing of these sounds to read words.

SSP is a highly structured approach that ensures that no phonics elements are left out and each new skill builds upon previously learned skills. This approach is widely considered effective for phonics instruction and is used in many educational systems.

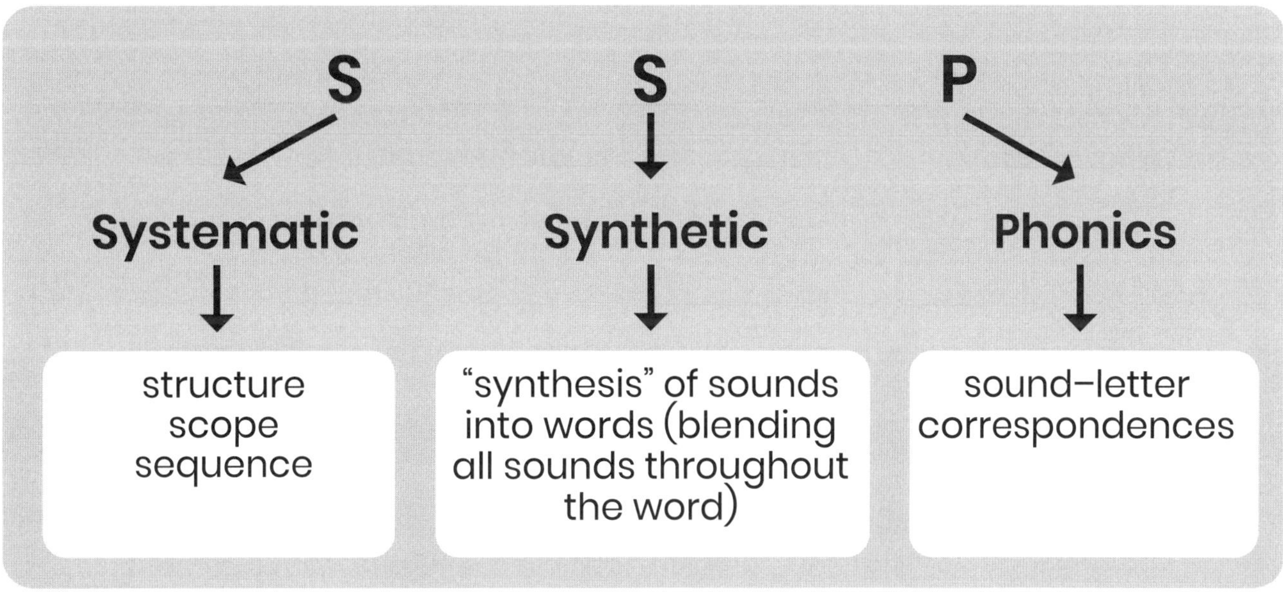

Systematic phonics in reading instruction

Teaching reading through systematic phonics is important because of the complexity of the English Alphabetic Code. To navigate this complexity, teachers should employ a scaffolded pedagogical framework:

- simple to complex: starting with the most basic elements and gradually introducing more challenging concepts
- stair-step progression
- systematic scope and sequence
- practice and consolidation along the way
- cumulative teaching

This methodical approach ensures that learners have a solid foundation, enabling them to confidently tackle the complexities of reading.

PHONEMIC AWARENESS AND READING STRATEGIES

Phonemic awareness: why it matters

Phonemic awareness is a pivotal skill for beginner readers that will play an important role in their journey towards literacy. Research has shown that phonics and phonemic awareness grow in tandem, and the most effective reading instruction teaches phonemic awareness with phonics.

The Simple View of Reading

The Simple View of Reading is a model that demonstrates the view that reading has two basic components: word recognition and language comprehension. This model offers a clear and effective framework for reading instruction.

The use of decodable books, the interaction between teachers, parents, and students, and the transition from learning to read to reading to learn are crucial elements of the Simple View of Reading approach. They shape how students progress towards independent reading across various texts and subjects.

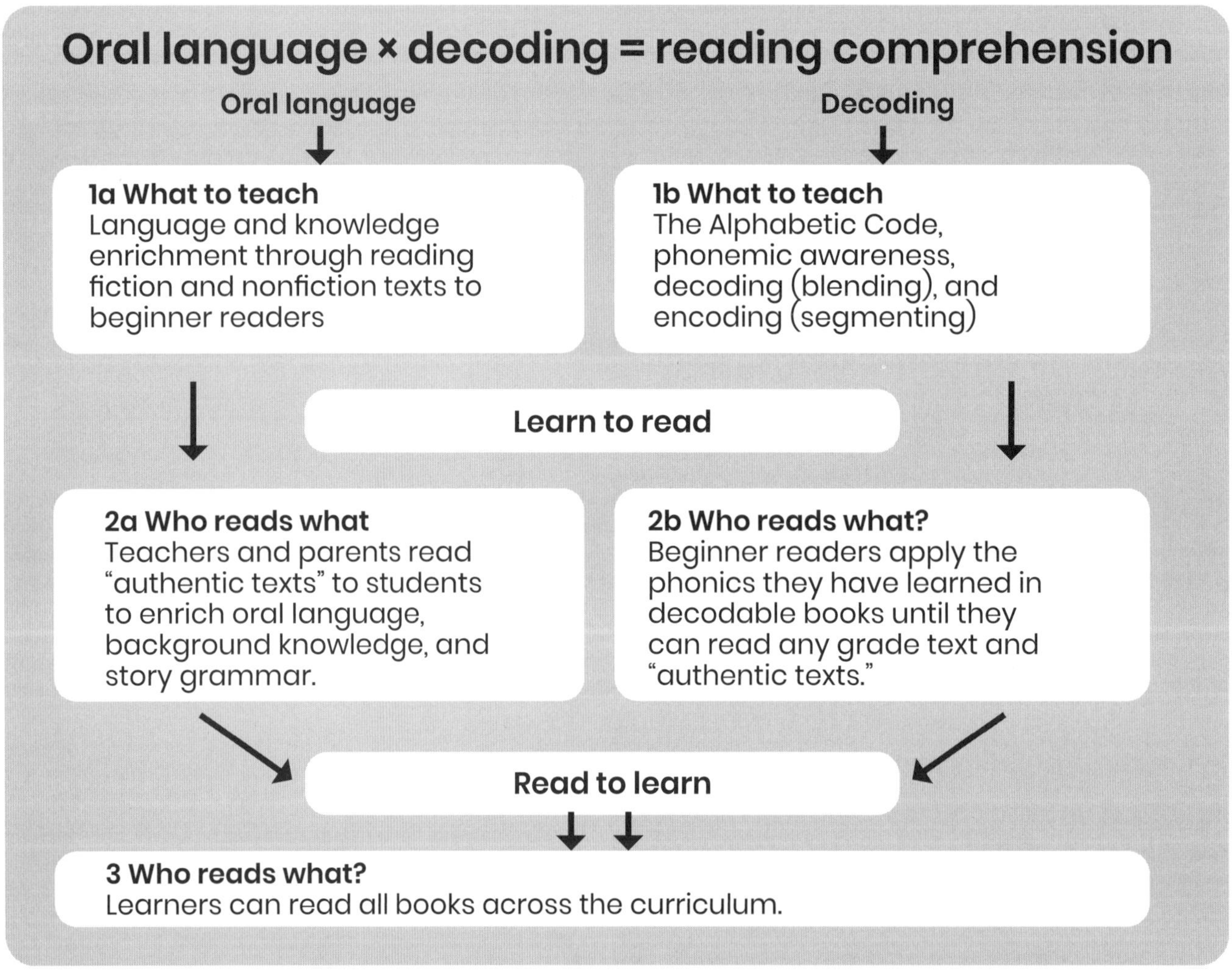

3-cueing vs decoding

The benefits of **3-cueing** versus **decoding strategies** is the subject of ongoing debate in literacy education. While 3-cueing focuses on using context and visual cues to identify words, decoding emphasizes the systematic breaking down of words into their phonetic components.

Decoding is increasingly recognized for its effectiveness in developing strong, foundational reading skills. This approach is grounded in systematic phonics and equips learners with the tools to tackle new and complex words independently. Conversely, 3-cueing relies on guessing that can lead the reader away from the text.

INSTRUCTIONAL MATERIALS

The role of decodable books in reading instruction

Practical application

Decodable books serve as practical tools where students apply their phonics knowledge in a controlled text. They offer students an opportunity to practice the phonic knowledge and skills they have learned. When students are taught mathematics, they are given exercises to practice what they have been taught, in order to internalize the new learning and to develop automaticity. Decodable texts perform a similar role in reading instruction.

Strategy and success

Based on the Science of Reading, decodable books focus on the decoding of graphemes and blending them into words, which steers students away from guessing. The controlled vocabulary is tailored to the phonic skills of the students, providing immediate reading success and boosting their confidence.

Focusing on a target phoneme (sound) or grapheme (spelling)

Decodable books target specific phoneme–grapheme correspondences, allowing students to practice reading with a focus on newly taught sounds and spellings. As students progress, the complexity of words in these books increases, and they start to look similar to more traditional reading books.

Motivation and independence

The sense of achievement students gain from successfully reading these books increases their motivation to continue learning to read, embodying the sentiment, "I can do this!"

Detractors of decodable books confuse the purpose of these books. They are not created to compete with wonderful children's literature, but are used for only a short time, as "training wheels" to help children develop good decoding skills. As students' proficiency in decoding grows, these supports can be removed, enabling them to take off and explore more complex reading materials.

3-cueing approach
a guessing strategy that leads the reader away from the text

Shep ran and hid in a shrub.

5

Guess the word.
1. Look at the picture.
2. What could it be? (bush? hedge?)
3. What is the first sound in the word?

Decoding approach
a strategy that focuses on letter-sound correspondences in words

Shep ran and hid in a shrub.

5

Read the word.
Sound out the letters and blend the sounds into a word.
/sh/ /r/ /u/ /b/ → "shrub"

THE PHONIC BOOKS PROGRAM

METHODOLOGY

The principles underlying our books are based on current thinking in the **Science of Reading**. We believe that all students can learn to read, and the best way to achieve this is by teaching them how the English writing system works by following a systematic approach. Written English is based on an alphabetic code that students need to unlock. Teaching students to recognize these graphemes and how to sound them and blend them into words is the route to reading success.

Our books and resources develop the five pillars of learning to read:

1. phonemic awareness
2. phonics
3. vocabulary
4. fluency
5. comprehension

At a later stage, students need to learn about morphemes (units of meaning) to enhance their vocabulary and comprehension.

Our books follow a systematic phonics approach. Starting by introducing only a few letters and sounds at a time, the reader can experience success from the very beginning. Our program teaches the following reading skills using explicit systematic phonics.

BLENDING AND SEGMENTING

Students learning to read with explicit systematic phonics are encouraged to sound out letters in words and push the sounds together into words. This is called **blending**. Each letter is sounded out separately and blended from left to right, throughout the word. This is the most reliable strategy to read a new word.

It's helpful for beginner readers to blend using "continuant" consonant sounds (e.g. /m/, /n/, /l/, /r/, and /s/) because these sounds are easier to prolong and blend together smoothly.

Students learn that spelling is the reverse activity of blending. When spelling, they learn to isolate each sound in the word and represent it with a spelling. This is called **segmenting**.

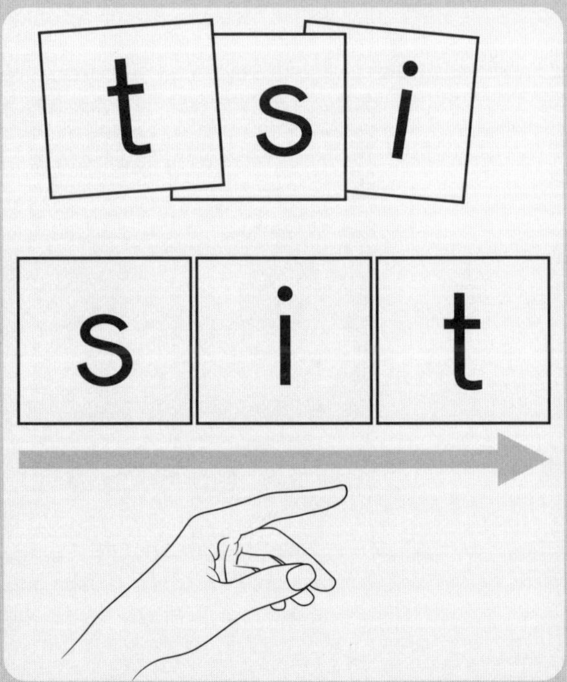

PHONEME MANIPULATION

Students learn to identify and isolate phonemes in words and to manipulate them by deleting, adding or swapping sounds in the words. This skill helps the reader to self-correct when making errors in reading.

Once students have been taught letter–sound correspondences, they can practice this new knowledge within controlled **decodable texts**. This means that students can sound out words that they can't yet read. Decodable texts encourage students to use "blending" sounds into words as the first strategy when reading, using the phonics they have been taught.

Learning a new skill takes a lot of practice so our books for beginner readers include games to practice reading words in the book. Our Dandelion Readers offer a **reading practice page** to ensure a successful reading experience of the text in the book.

All our books have cumulative progression which allows for previous learning to be included as the reader progresses. This ensures what has been learned is included and practiced along the way.

Students learn new **vocabulary** through reading and our books offer an opportunity for this. As they learn to decode a growing number of words, new words are introduced which will help them develop their language skills.

The **activity books** are a supplementary resource to support students who need extra practice at each level. Although our books can be used independently, we recommend using the activity books alongside to enhance and consolidate learning. Some activities, such as blending, segmenting, and phoneme manipulation precede the books, whereas others are directly linked to the books in the corresponding series and are designed to develop reading fluency, spelling, writing, and comprehension skills.

PROGRAM OVERVIEW

In line with explicit systematic phonics and the Science of Reading, our books offerstair-step phonics progression for Kindergarten, starting from the simple to the more complex parts of the Alphabetic Code.

There are three distinct series of Dandelion decodable books that cover the sounds of the alphabet and double consonants: Dandelion Launchers, Dandelion Launchers Extras, and Dandelion World. Consistent in their scope and sequence, these series start by introducing only a few sounds and letters at a time (Stage 1 introduces only five sounds: s, a, t, i, m), ensuring students can experience success from the outset.

Additionally, the Dandelion Readers Sets 1–3 readers follow a similar progression but with more text per page, catering to more advanced beginner learners. Furthermore our Dandelion Readers VCe series, provides coverage of the silent 'e' patterns a–e, e–e, i–e, o–e, and u–e, ensuring that students are well-equipped to tackle these more challenging phonics rules. This systematic, step-by-step methodology is crucial for developing confident and proficient readers.

Dandelion Launchers

This series is a fully decodable phonic series for beginner readers. Each pair of books in the series introduces only a few letters/sounds at a time, which allows for independent reading from the beginning. The series provides practice while offering different stories, with each stage introducing new letters/sounds and reviewing previously taught letters/ sounds and high-frequency words. A game is included at the back of each book, offering a fun way to practice the new phonic skills and knowledge introduced at each stage.

Dandelion Launchers Extras

These books are designed to complement the Dandelion Launchers series, providing additional practice for the sounds of the alphabet at CVC (Consonant–Vowel–Consonant) level. They follow the same cumulative scope and sequence as the original Dandelion Launchers series, meaning they progress in the same way and cover the same content. The Extras series includes 30 different readers that aim to reinforce the learning by introducing only a few letters/sounds at a time, similar to the original series, but with different stories.

Dandelion World

Dandelion World is the parallel series to Dandelion Launchers and covers a range of engaging nonfiction topics. Each book includes a nonfiction knowledge builder feature for children and adults to read together. This is a fun way to enhance vocabulary and deepen comprehension of the book's content.

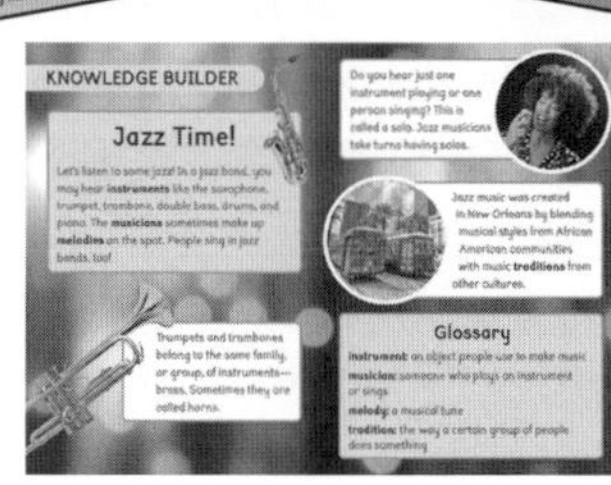

Dandelion Readers Sets 1–3

The Dandelion Readers Sets 1–3 are three series of books that follow a similar progression found in Dandelion Launchers. These series feature a greater amount of text on each page, with the text volume progressively increasing throughout each series. While this manual does not include specific lesson plans for these series, they can be used as supplementary materials for your lessons.

Dandelion Readers VCe Series / Dandelion World VCe Series

The Dandelion Readers VCe Series is a series of decodable books that specifically targets the silent 'e' spellings in the English language. Aimed at advancing beginner readers, this series introduces the key VCe (Vowel-Consonant-e) spellings, a–e, e–e, i–e, o–e, and u–e, through various engaging and illustrated stories. Each book in the series focuses on one VCe spelling pattern at a time, ensuring that students can gradually master these spelling conventions. There is also a corresponding Dandelion World VCe series of nonfiction readers, which follows the same scope and sequence.

Activity books

Each series has accompanying activity books. These books are integral to the reading program, as they include teaching and practice activities to support the learner.

PROGRAM FEATURES

The Phonic Books program for Kindergarten is designed to engage beginner readers by offering a range of features tailored to support reading success and build confidence.

- **Engaging content:** the program includes engaging nonfiction texts and imaginative stories featuring appealing characters that captivate young readers. The text is designed to be engaging, ensuring that readers remain engaged and motivated.
- **Accessible design:** the books use a dyslexia-friendly font and present text on suitable backgrounds, making them more accessible and easier to read.
- **Structured progression:** a highly structured sequence carefully guides the student from simple to more complex phonics concepts.
- **Cumulative learning:** the books follow a cumulative progression, ensuring that previously learned phonics skills are revisited and reinforced.
- **High-frequency words:** the program gradually introduces high-frequency words.
- **Decodable texts:** the program uses controlled decodable texts that allow students to apply their phonic knowledge to reading texts.
- **Vocabulary development:** as students' decoding skills improve, new words are introduced to help develop their language skills.
- **Interactive games and activities:** the program also offers a variety of games and activities, such as fishing games, snap cards, and dice games, to make learning more interactive and enjoyable, while helping to consolidate learning.
- **Activity books:** accompanying activity books are available to reinforce the skills learned in the books. These books are designed to support reading fluency, spelling, writing, and comprehension skills.
- **Free printable resources:** a range of free printable reading and spelling sources are available on the Phonic Books website.

CURRICULUM ALIGNMENT

Our books can be used to complement any phonics program once the students have been taught the letters/sounds in the books. However, they follow the progression of the **Sounds-Write® Reading and Spelling Program**. Curriculum mapping grids for Kindergarten can be found on our website.

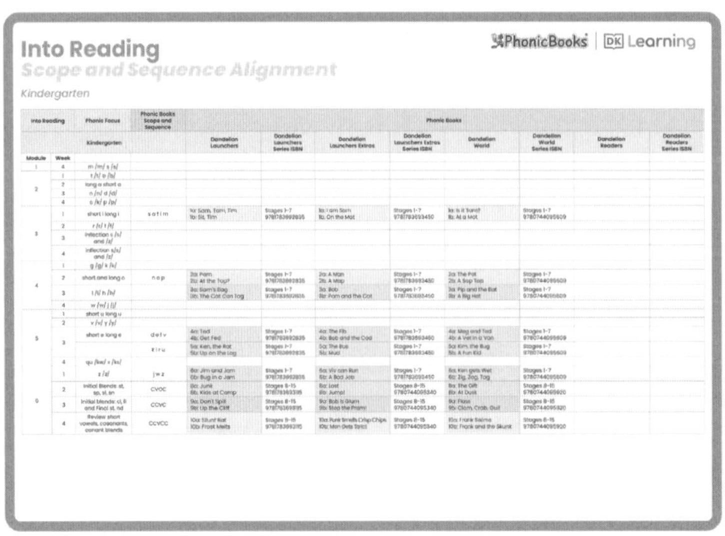

SCOPE AND SEQUENCE

The scope and sequence provided below offers a detailed overview of our Phonic Books program for Kindergarten level readers. It outlines each stage of the curriculum, detailing the specific book titles that cover each stage. It also highlights the corresponding parallel series that focus on the same phonic skills, which can be used for additional practice. These parallel series present varied contexts, ranging from diverse storylines to informative nonfiction texts, as exemplified by the Dandelion World series. The tables also specify the word structures covered at each stage, such as CVC words for the first seven stages. This structured approach is designed to present teachers with a clear roadmap of the program's progression.

Stages 1–7

Dandelion Launchers	**Dandelion Launchers Extras**	**Dandelion World**	**Stage**	**Phonic focus**	**Word structure**
Book 1a: Sam, Tam, Tim Book 1b: Is it Sam?	Book 1a: I am Sam Book 1b: On the Mat	Book 1a: Sit, Tim Book 1b: At a Mat	1	s a t i m	CVC
Book 2a: Pam Book 2b: The Pot	Book 2a: A Man Book 2b: A Map	Book 2a: At the Top? Book 2b: A Sap Tap	2	n o p	
Book 3a: Sam's Bag Book 3b: Pip and the Bat	Book 3a: Bob Book 3b: Pam and the Cat	Book 3a: The Cat Can Tag Book 3b: A Big Hat	3	b c g h	
Book 4a: Ted Book 4b: Meg and Ted	Book 4a: The Fib Book 4b: Bob and the Cod	Book 4a: Get Fed Book 4b: A Vet in a Van	4	d e f v	
Book 5a: Ken, the Rat Book 5b: Kim, the Bug	Book 5a: The Bus Book 5b: Mud	Book 5a: Up on the Log Book 5b: A Fun Kid	5	k l r u	
Book 6a: Jim and Jam Book 6b: Ken Gets Wet	Book 6a: Viv Can Run Book 6b: A Bad Job	Book 6a: Bug in a Jam Book 6b: Zig, Zag, Tag	6	j w z	
Book 7a: Rex Yells Book 7b: Rex Will Not Sit	Book 7a: Bob on the Sill Book 7b: The Hill	Book 7a: The Jazz Gig Book 7b: In the Dell	7	x y ff ll ss zz	

Stages 8–15

Dandelion Launchers	Dandelion Launchers Extras	Dandelion World	Stage	Phonic focus and skill focus
Book 8a: Junk Book 8b: The Gift	Book 8a: Lost Book 8b: Jump!	Book 8a: Kids at Camp Book 8b: At Dusk	8	CVCC
Book 9a: Don't Spill Book 9b: Floss	Book 9a: Bob is Glum Book 9b: Stop the Pram!	Book 9a: Up the Cliff Book 9b: Clam, Crab, Gull	9	CCVC
Book 10a: Stunt Rat Book 10b: Frank Swims	Book 10a: Punk Smells Crisp Chips Book 10b: Mom Gets Strict	Book 10a: Frost Melts Book 10b: Frank and the Skunk	10	CCVCC
Book 11a: Nuts for Lunch Book 11b: The Champ	Book 11a: The Big Chip Book 11b: Chit Chat	Book 11a: Crunch, Munch! Book 11b: Chimp Chums	11	ch
Book 12a: Shep and Tosh Book 12b: Fresh Fish	Book 12a: The Shop Book 12b: The Fish Pond	Book 12a: Trash in the Trench Book 12b: Sled Dogs Dash	12	sh
Book 13a: This and That Book 13b: Will This Fit?	Book 13a: Thud! Crash! Book 13b: That's It!	Book 13a: Sloths Book 13b: The Thrill of a Run	13	th
Book 14a: The Back Pack Book 14b: Which Shall I Pick?	Book 14a: The Clock Book 14b: When Can I Get On?	Book 14a: Shells and Rocks Book 14b: Flick the Puck	14	ck, wh
Book 15a: Ding Dong! Book 15b: The Strong Wind	Book 15a: Spring Book 15b: Ting-a-ling	Book 15a: Spring Has Sprung Book 15b: Long Bat Wings	15	ng, qu

***Dandelion Readers* Sets 1–3**

Set 1 Units 1–10	Set 2 Units 1–10	Set 3 Units 1–10	Phonic focus and skill level
Book 1: Sam	Book 1: Sam and Tim	Book 1: Sit on It	s a t i m
Book 2: Pip	Book 2: The Nap	Book 2: Pip, Sam, and Tam	n o p
Book 3: In the Bag	Book 3: In the Can	Book 3: A Hot Cab	b c g h
Book 4: Bad Cat	Book 4: At the Vet	Book 4: In the Van	d e f v
Book 5: Bun in the Sun	Book 5: Red Gum	Book 5: The Hut	k l r u
Book 6: Zip and Zap	Book 6: Meg and the Bun	Book 6: Top Dog	j w z
Book 7: Bob Is Not Well	Book 7: Up a Big Hill	Book 7: I Will Sell	x y ff ll ss zz
Book 8: The Lost Box	Book 8: Lost in the Pond	Book 8: The Best Gift	VCC CVCC
Book 9: Flip and Flop Slip	Book 9: The Trap	Book 9: Fred Has a Plan	CCVC
Book 10: The Stink	Book 10: Punk and the Plums	Book 10: The Stilts	CCVCC

Dandelion Readers Sets 11–15

Set 1 Units 11–15	Set 2 Units 11–15	Phonic focus and skill level
Book 11: Pip Gets Rich	Book 11: Twin Chimps	ch
Book 12: "Hush!"	Book 12: The Cash	sh
Book 13: The Path Up the Hill	Book 13: Thump, Thump	th
Book 14: The Trick	Book 14: Raj Gets a Shock	ck
Book 15: The Ring	Book 15: The Sting	ng
Book 16: The Quest	Book 16: The Quilt	qu ve

Dandelion Readers VCe Spellings

VCe Spellings Books 1–6	Phonic focus and/or skill level
Book 1: Late	a–e
Book 2: Pete	e–e
Book 3: A Fine Life	i–e
Book 4: The Note	o–e
Book 5: Club Rules	u–e
Book 6: Show Time	a–e, e–e, i–e, o–e, u–e

GETTING STARTED

Start by reviewing the scheme of work charts outlined in the next section. These are designed to provide an easy-to-navigate and in-depth understanding of the entire Phonic Books program for Kindergarten. They will guide you through the program's progression, detailing the sequence in which phonemes and graphemes are introduced in each lesson plan. Each lesson plan specifies which phonic skills are being developed to ensure a systematic approach to learning. The charts are organized by series and include several key components: the phonic focus for each lesson plan, lesson objectives, order of steps, high-frequency words, vocabulary lists, and lesson resources. Recommendations are given for when to conduct reading assessments to track students' progress. Whether planning lessons, tracking a student's progress, or understanding the journey ahead, the scheme of work charts are a useful reference.

Next, move on to the lesson structure and teaching methods section. The lesson structure section explains the program's lesson framework, including the pattern of activities and methods used for effective teaching. Each lesson plan is divided into five distinct lessons. Explanations are provided on how the lessons are structured and the purpose of the different lesson elements are explained. The teaching methods section that follows explains how to teach the core lesson activities and uses examples from the activity books to illustrate how the resources can be integrated into the lessons.

The differentiation section on page 50 provides guidance on how to tailor lessons to meet diverse student needs. It provides strategies for using the activity book resources to create customizable lessons, including support for the lowest attaining 20% of students, those with special educational needs, and students for whom English is a second language.

Lastly, regular student assessment is important for enhancing both learning and teaching. The lesson plans incorporate formative assessments through various activities and games. However, periodic summative assessments are also an important tool for gauging student progress. Refer to the section on reading assessments (page 52) for guidance on when and how to conduct these assessments.

After reviewing these sections, you are now ready to proceed with the main lesson plans of the program, which begin on page 90.

SCHEMES OF WORK

Stages 1–7: Sounds of the alphabet

Lesson plan	Objectives	High-frequency words	Resources
Stage 1: s, a, t, i, m	In this first lesson plan, students will learn to accurately read new words by applying the phonic sounds /s/, /a/, /t/, /i/, and /m/. They will focus on blending these sounds to form and recognize simple CVC words.	n/a	Dandelion Launchers Stages 1–7: Book 1a: Sam, Tam, Tim Dandelion Launchers Stages 1–7 Activities
Stage 2: n, o, p	In subsequent lesson plans, students will consolidate previously learned sounds and learn new sounds. In this lesson plan, students will: • review /s/, /a/, /t/, /i/, and /m/ • read new words using the sounds /n/, /o/, and /p/	I, is, a	Dandelion Launchers Stages 1–7: Book 2a: Pam Dandelion Launchers Stages 1–7 Activities
Stage 3: b, c, g, h	Students will: • review /s/, /a/, /t/, /i/, /m/, /n/, /o/, and /p/ • read new words using the sounds /b/, /c/, /g/, and /h/	Sam's, has, a, get, the, is, Tam's	Dandelion Launchers Stages 1–7: Book 3a: Sam's Bag Dandelion Launchers Stages 1–7 Activities
Stage 4: d, e, f, v	Students will: • review /s/, /a/, /t/, /i/, /m/, /n/, /o/, /p/, /b/, /c/, /g/, and /h/ • read new words using the sounds /d/, /e/, /f/, and /v/	the, up, off, into, is, a	Dandelion Launchers Stages 1–7: Book 4a: Ted Dandelion Launchers Stages 1–7 Activities
Stage 5: k, l, r, u	Students will: • review /s/, /a/, /t/, /i/, /m/, /n/, /o/, /p/, /b/, /c/, /g/, /h/, /d/, /e/, /f/, and /v/ • read new words using the sounds /k/, /l/, /r/, and /u/	the, a, it's	Dandelion Launchers Stages 1–7: Book 5a: Ken, the Rat Dandelion Launchers Stages 1–7 Activities
Stage 6: j, w, z	Students will: • review /s/, /a/, /t/, /i/, /m/, /n/, /o/, /p/, /b/, /c/, /g/, /h/, /d/, /e/, /f/, /v/, /k/, /l/, /r/, and /u/ • read new words using the sounds /j/, /w/, and /z/	and, was, his, I, have, a, of, to, the, legs, into	Dandelion Launchers Stages 1–7: Book 6a: Jim and Jam Dandelion Launchers Stages 1–7 Activities
Stage 7: x, y, ff, ll, ss, zz	Students will: • review /s/, /a/, /t/, /i/, /m/, /n/, /o/, /p/, /b/, /c/, /g/, /h/, /d/, /e/, /f/, /v/, /k/, /l/, /r/, /u/, /w/, and /z/ • read new words using the sounds /x/, /y/, /ff/, /ll/, /ss/, and /zz/	yells, I, the, and, was, no, be, a, said	Dandelion Launchers Stages 1–7: Book 7a: Rex Yells Dandelion Launchers Stages 1–7 Activities

Stages 8–15: Consonant blends and digraphs

Lesson plan	Objectives	High-frequency words	Resources
Stage 8: CVCC	Students will learn to blend and segment consonants and vowels to read and write CVCC words, focusing on the incorporation of previously learned sounds.	I, of, this, old, said, to, the, that	Dandelion Launchers Stages 8–15: Book 8a: Junk Dandelion Launchers Stages 8–15 Activities
Stage 9: CCVC	Using their knowledge of previously learned sounds, students will focus on creating and decoding words with initial consonant blends such as 'bl,' 'cr,' 'st,' and 'fl.'	we, have, a, of, don't, says, the, to, is	Dandelion Launchers Stages 8–15: Book 9a: Don't Spill Dandelion Launchers Stages 8–15 Activities
Stage 10: CCVCC	Students will build on their skills by learning and practicing words with CCVCC word structures, such as "print."	is, he, as, I, be, a, says, the	Dandelion Launchers Stages 8–15: Book 10a: Stunt Rat Dandelion Launchers Stages 8–15 Activities
Stage 11: ch	Students are introduced to the consonant digraph /ch/ and will learn how to read and write it in various words.	a, was, to, the, for, his, I, have, said, plant, of	Dandelion Launchers Stages 8–15: Book 11a: Nuts for Lunch Dandelion Launchers Stages 8–15 Activities
Stage 12: sh	Students are introduced to the consonant digraph /sh/ and will learn how to read and write it in various words.	I, a, was, you, be, my, to, no, yelled, said	Dandelion Launchers Stages 8–15: Book 12a: Shep and Tosh Dandelion Launchers Stages 8–15 Activities
Stage 13: th	Students are introduced to the consonant digraph /th/ and will learn how to read and write it in various words.	to, I, have, a, of, the	Dandelion Launchers Stages 8–15: Book 13a: This and That Dandelion Launchers Stages 8–15 Activities
Stage 14: ck, wh	Students will expand their phonic skills by learning new digraphs /ck/ and /wh/.	the, for, says, you, a, is, have	Dandelion Launchers Stages 8–15: Book 14a: The Back Pack Dandelion Launchers Stages 8–15 Activities
Stage 15: ng, qu	Students will expand their phonic skills by learning new digraphs /ng/ and /qu/.	is, the, I, have, a, of, happy birthday, to, you	Dandelion Launchers Stages 8–15: Book 15a: Ding Dong! Dandelion Launchers Stages 8–15 Activities

Dandelion Readers VCe Spellings

Lesson plan	Objectives	High-frequency words	New vocabulary	Resources
a–e	Students will learn and practice the 'a–e' spelling for the sound /ae/ (e.g. "**l**a**te**"). In this and subsequent lesson plans, reading practice pages and games help to consolidate learning, reading practice pages and games help to consolidate learning.	was, he, for, school, birthday, no, said, the, his, they, she, goal, day	shame, blame	Dandelion Readers, VCe Spellings Book 1: Late VCe Spellings Activities
e–e	Students will learn and practice the 'e–e' spelling for the sound /ee/ (e.g. "th**e**m**e**").	is, I'll, make, to, said, his, he, the, began, boots, no, do	complete, completed, concrete, extremely	Dandelion Readers, VCe Spellings Book 2: Pete VCe Spellings Activities
i–e	Students will learn and practice the 'i–e' spelling for the sound /ie/ (e.g. "f**i**n**e**").	his, were, little, they, lived, of, leaves, he, to, the, we, my, said, politely, be, baby	fine, hive, politely, stack	Dandelion Readers, VCe Spellings Book 3: A Fine Life VCe Spellings Activities
o–e	Students will learn and practice the 'o–e' spelling for the sound /o e/ (e.g. "r**o**p**e**").	the, Toad, he, saw, said, follow, to, onto, was, into, my, hello, you, have, me	task, cope	Dandelion Readers, VCe Spellings Book 4: The Note VCe Spellings Activities
u–e	Students will learn and practice that the VCe spelling 'u–e' can represent two sounds: /oo/ as in "r**u**d**e**" and /ue/ as in "c**u**t**e**".	play, said, we, the, they, to, began, cheat, you, are, by, I, again	accuse, refuse, brute, include	Dandelion Readers, VCe Spellings Book 5: Club Rules VCe Spellings Activities
a–e, e–e, i–e, o–e, u–e	Students will consolidate their understanding of VCe patterns by practicing these previously learned patterns in different words.	show, said, the, robot, say, who, of, began, play, he, put, his, I, they, as, was, to, all, were, give	compete, throne, graceful, advice	Dandelion Readers, VCe Spellings Book 6: Show Time VCe Spellings Activities

LESSON PLAN STRUCTURE

Each lesson plan is divided into five distinct steps, focusing on:

1. Preparation
2. Application for reading
3. Application for writing
4. Comprehension and consolidation
5. Tracking progress

A typical lesson plan follows the structured format below, though not every lesson will follow this exact structure. Lessons or activities should be offered daily, when possible, and last not more than 15 minutes for younger students.

Step 1: Preparation

In this first step, the teacher begins by outlining the goal of the lesson plan: learning the new sounds and reinforcing previously learned ones. Spend a couple of minutes introducing these new sounds and the story that will be central to teaching the upcoming lessons. Then demonstrate the correct pronunciation of these sounds. **Sound cards** or **Word-building cards** from the activity books can be effective in modeling the new sounds, making the lesson more engaging and interactive.

Following the introduction, move on to a word-building activity. The students listen to the sounds in each word and then build the words using sound cards or magnetic letters, and with the aid of picture cards. The objective is for students to construct words corresponding to the pictures by employing the sounds they have learned. It's important that students focus on the sounds first, then find the letters that represent these sounds. This reinforces the link between phonemic awareness and written language.

The next phase of the lesson focuses on segmenting and blending sounds in words. A multisensory approach is effective for teaching. Use gestures to aid learning like pointing to the letters as they are sounded out and using a swishing motion with your finger for blending. This helps for transitioning to spelling activities, which link phonic skills with reading and writing.

This first step typically concludes with a word chain activity, incorporating both real and nonsense words. This activity is designed to reinforce the concepts taught in the lesson, while also being fun and interactive.

Step 2: Application for reading

In the second step, students apply their phonic skills by reading a decodable text. They are encouraged to sound out the words and blend them together. When the reading is laborious, the teacher can reread the sentence after the students to help them comprehend the text. Ensure that any new vocabulary is discussed and explained.

The Phonic Books lesson plans in this instructional manual suggest that reading the story should take the form of a directed reading by the teacher. However, a number of options for teachers reading the book are also recommended:

- The teacher reads the book and students follow.
- Students engage in choral reading.
- Students engage in individual whisper reading while the teacher circulates and listens to each student.
- Students participate in paired reading, taking turns reading to one another—either by reading and rereading the books or by taking turns to read alternate pages.

It is important to emphasize that students must have an opportunity to read to the teacher individually so that they engage actively with the text and the teacher can offer error correction. This is also the time when the teacher can assess their decoding skills and their phonic knowledge.

For extension, as students progress through the program and learn to read more fluently, the teachers can support students to read with expression and prosody.
For example, adjusting their pitch, pace, and emphasis. This helps students to improve their reading fluency, improve their understanding of texts, and make reading more enjoyable.

Step 3: Application for spelling

To strengthen letter formation skills, it is important to integrate multisensory activities early on. Before progressing to writing complete words like "sit," ensure students have practiced forming individual letters such as 's,' 'a,' 't,' 'i,' and 'm.' This can include activities like skywriting, where students trace the letters in the air while saying the corresponding sounds, and practicing writing each letter multiple times before attempting to write words.

Letter formation activities are not provided in the lesson plans in this manual. Students should have regular opportunities throughout the weeks to practice forming letters correctly, ensuring they are adequately prepared for writing tasks involving complete words.

In this step, students practice writing the graphemes they have learned in the previous lessons. The teacher should encourage the students to say the sounds as they write them and to blend the sounds in each word together.

Following this, the students can progress to writing entire words. Students can engage in various activities designed to reinforce this skill. For instance, they might participate in exercises like **Fill in all the missing sounds** activity, which challenges students to identify and write the missing sounds in words.

Additionally, the activity books include **Sentence dictation** activities. During these activities, students should be encouraged to sound out each word as they spell it. This practice not only enhances their spelling skills but also reinforces their understanding of how individual sounds come together to form words within the context of a sentence.

Step 4: Comprehension and consolidation

In this step, the teacher revisits the story, reading it aloud to help students consolidate their understanding.

Following the reading, students engage in a variety of comprehension activities. For example, the **Retelling the story** activity found in the activity books contains pictures and words on a photocopiable page. Students retell the story or create their own story using the pictures and word cards provided. Additional comprehension exercises are also available in the activity books, offering a range of options for further reading practice or support.

Step 5: Tracking progress

In this final step, the focus shifts to monitoring and assessing the progress students have made with the new phonic skills and sounds they have learned.
To facilitate this, teachers can draw from a range of activities designed for formative assessments.

For example, the **Bookmark** in the activity books contains lists of words that can be used for practicing reading and spelling. Teachers can use these bookmarks to conduct quick, formative assessments of each student's progress.

Additionally, the Dandelion Launchers series of activity books include **Reading certificates**. These can be used to track each student's progress through the reading stages, and they also help to encourage and motivate the students.

Stages 8–15 introduces a **Spelling assessment** activity at the end of each stage. Use these to assess students' ability to spell the sounds they have learned.

Additional activities to supplement lessons

Additional activities can be found in the activity books and online teaching resources. These can be used to widen literacy development, but they also offer the flexibility to create differentiated lessons to meet the diverse needs of students. They can be used to address gaps in understanding, enhance punctuation and comprehension skills, or provide extension for more advanced students. Here are some examples.

Matching upper to lower case/Fishing game: These activities can be used for teaching and practicing recognition of lower case and upper case letters.

Punctuation: Introduced in the VCe Spellings Activities, this activity involves giving students an extract from a story with missing capital letters and periods. Students identify the correct placement and quantity of these punctuation marks. This exercise is useful for reinforcing punctuation rules and writing skills.

Word trail cards: This activity features pictures and words to offer an interactive reading activity. Students find and read the corresponding word to each picture, thereby promoting word recognition and reading fluency. It also helps to build sequencing skills as students follow the trail from one card to the next.

Timed reading: This activity involves students reading a series of words as quickly as they can, recording their times in three attempts. This repetitive practice can help to improve a student's reading pace and fluency.

Reading practice cards: In the Dandelion Readers VCe Spellings Activities book, word cards are introduced for reading practice. These cards provide examples of words containing sounds the students have just learned. These pages can be photocopied for use in a matching game format or to introduce new vocabulary, offering a more structured approach to reading practice.

Stepping stones or **Reading game:** Using counters and dice, players read aloud words or letter sounds they land on during each turn. These games not only make learning fun but also provide practice in reading and phonic skills.

Four-in-a-row game: In this fun and interactive game, players read a word and place a counter on it, aiming to get four counters in a row (horizontally, vertically, or diagonally).

Splitting two-syllable words: Later in the program, students are introduced to two-syllable words. In this activity, students practice splitting words into syllables, writing each syllable, then reassembling them while vocalizing each syllable. This improves phonemic awareness and students' understanding of word structure.

Parallel books

Lesson plans for Stages 1–15 use the Dandelion Launchers series as the lesson resources; however, Phonic Books has parallel books in the same series and in the Dandelion Launchers Extras, Dandelion World, and Dandelion Readers Sets 1–3 that can be used to teach the same lessons. These alternative or supplementary resources are clearly indicated in the lesson plans, specifying which parallel books align with each lesson. This provides teachers with the flexibility to vary their teaching materials and cater to different preferences.

In the subsequent section on teaching methods, there is a more in-depth exploration of how to effectively implement these techniques. It includes specific references to the activity books and offers practical guidance on how to integrate these resources into a multisensory teaching approach.

TEACHING METHODS

This section expands on the teaching methods mentioned in the preceding section on lesson plan structure, connecting them to the program's activity books. It provides practical tips for integrating these methods and resources into your lessons. The figure below shows an example of an activity from one of the activity books.

The top of each page clearly indicates the specific stage and the phonic skills being targeted.

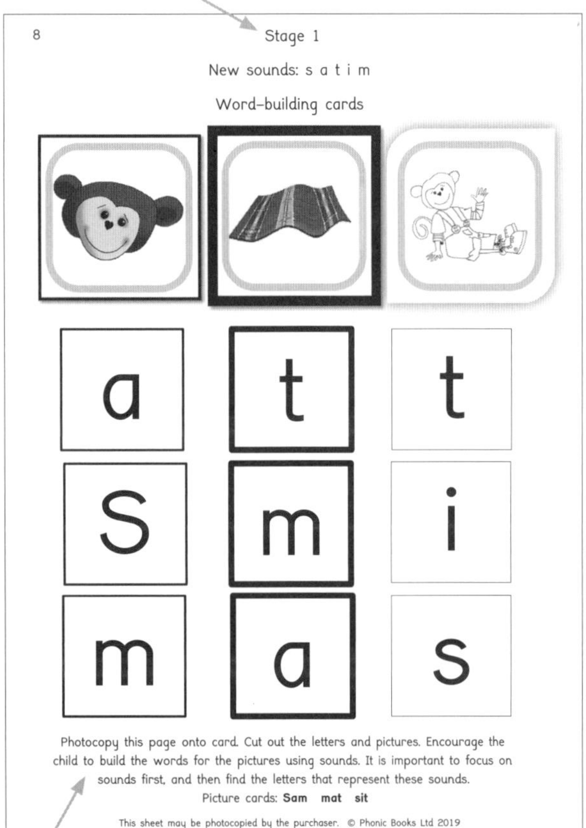

Teacher instructions at the bottom of the page offer step-by-step directions for teaching the activities.

Activities can be photocopied, allowing for widespread use for multiple students.

Introducing new letter sounds

In the Phonic Books program, multiple letter sounds are introduced in each lesson. This provides students with an immediate foundation for word creation. In the second and subsequent lesson plans, previously learned sounds should be reviewed in short bursts of revision.

An important part of this process is demonstrating the correct pronunciation of each sound, e.g. modeling the consonant sounds without the 'uh' sound: /m/ and not /muh/. Learning to pronounce the sounds precisely will help beginner readers to blend them into recognizable words.

After modeling the sound, encourage students to carefully watch and replicate the sound.

Employing a multisensory approach in teaching new letter sounds can improve the effectiveness of the learning process. Using **Sound cards** or **Word-building cards** from the activity books can be useful for modeling these new sounds.

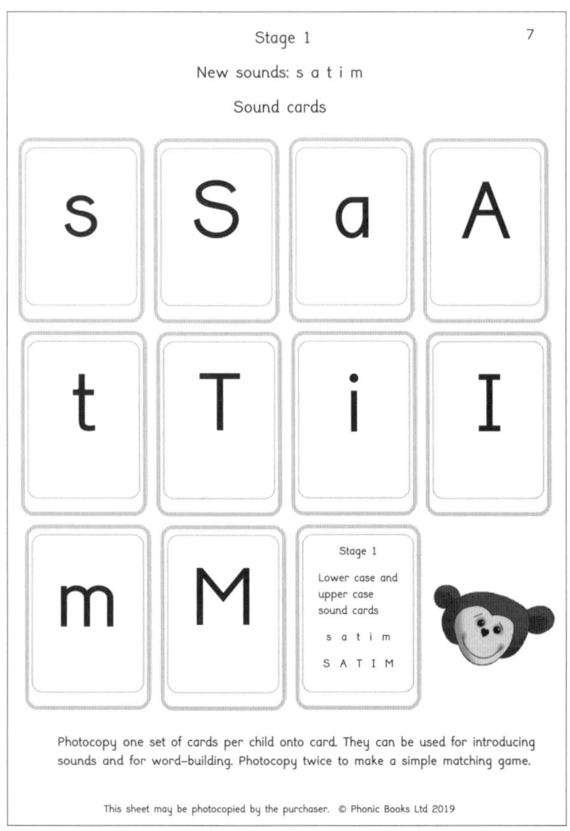

How to teach word building

Word building is the most effective activity to teach segmenting, blending, and spelling. Word building teaches segmenting with letters. **Segmenting** is the ability to separate sounds in words. The smallest sounds are called phonemes. We use segmenting when we sound out a new word, for example /k/ /a/ /t/ → "cat." We say the sounds separately and then we push them together to make a word.

We also use segmenting when we spell. When spelling the word "cat," we need to segment the word into the sounds /k/ /a/ /t/ and then spell those sounds with letters. Many programs introduce segmenting as an oral activity. For example, students listen to the sounds in words and then count them or place counters to represent the sounds.

While these activities may develop segmenting, they are not the most effective way to learn this skill. It is important to recognize that when we speak, we don't say all the sounds precisely. Many sounds get gobbled up, or clipped, and others change depending on where they are in the word.

Research has shown that teaching segmenting is more effective when introduced with letters. Oral segmenting is only a stepping stone that has no benefit on its own.

How to teach segmenting with letters

The most effective way of teaching segmenting is through a word-building activity. The teacher asks the student to build a word. This entails listening to the sounds in the word, placing the letters into the correct sequence, then sounding out the word and reading it. This should also be combined with writing the word as this links reading and spelling.

Step 1: Lines scaffold the word

Draw the number of lines on a whiteboard that correspond to the number of sounds in the word. In this example, draw three lines for the word "mat." Place the cards needed to build the word jumbled up above the lines.

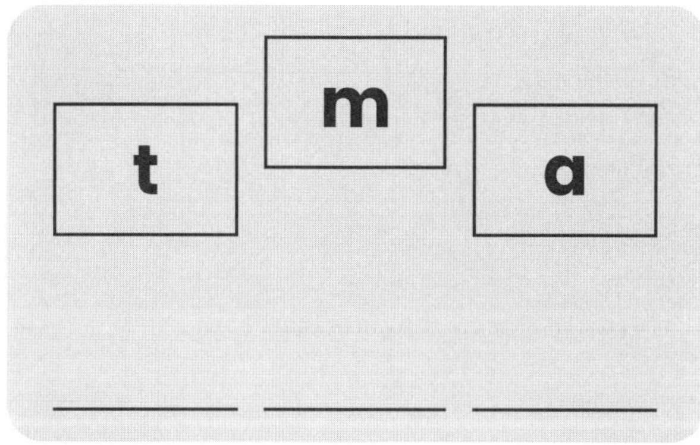

Step 2: Build the word

Tell the student that you are going to build the word "mat." Point to the first line and ask the student to listen to the first sound as you say the word slowly. Move your finger along the lines in sync with the sounds in the word.

When the student says /m/, ask them to bring down the letter for /m/ onto the first line. Repeat this process with the remaining letters/sounds in the word.

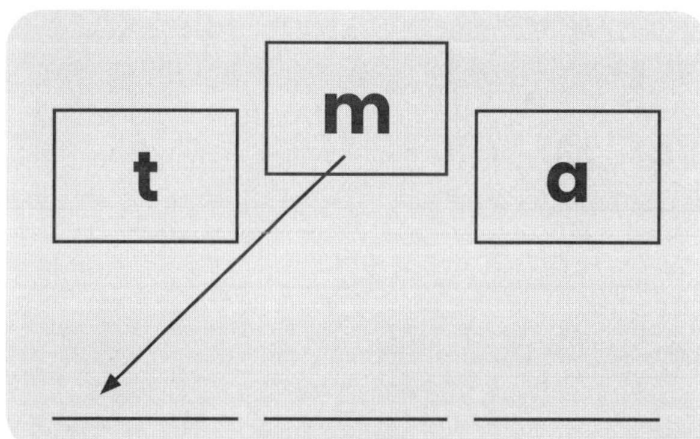

Step 3: Sound out and blend into the word

Now that the student has built the word, ask them to sound out the word and blend the sounds together into a word: /m/ /a/ /t/ → "mat."

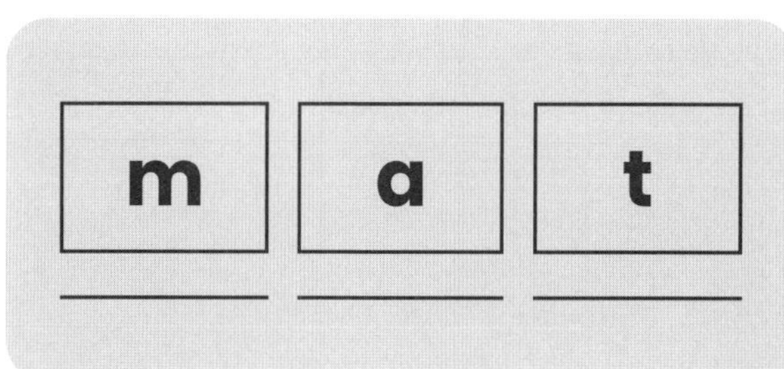

Step 4: Spell the word

Ask the student to spell the word under the lines and to say the sounds as they write each letter.

Finally, the student sounds out the word they have written and reads it.

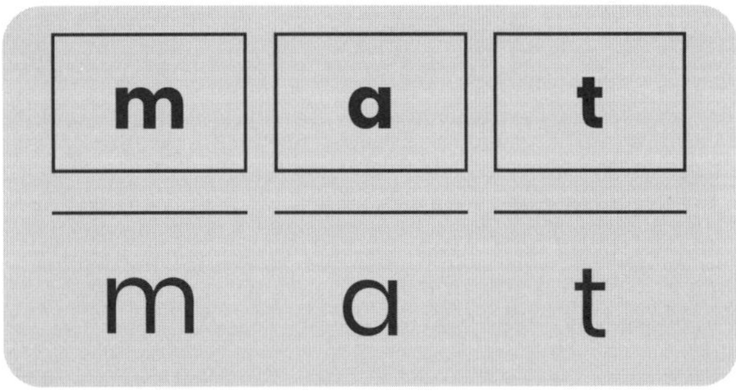

As you can see, word-building activities that use letters give the student a visual representation for the sounds in words. We show them the sequence of the sounds and how they are represented by letters. This is a direct and effective way of teaching segmenting and blending. It also demonstrates the link between reading and spelling in a clear way.

Word-building activities are a core feature of the activity books in the program. In the early stages, this activity takes the form of letters and picture cards, like in this example from Dandelion Launchers, Stage 1.

28

Stage 2

New sounds: n o p

Word-building cards

P p m
p t P
i o a

Photocopy this page onto card. Cut out the letters and pictures. Encourage the child to build the words for the pictures using sounds. It is important to focus on sounds first, and then find the letters that represent these sounds.
Picture cards: Pip pot Pam

This sheet may be photocopied by the purchaser. © Phonic Books Ltd 2019

As the program progresses, a more advanced word-building activity is introduced, as demonstrated in the example from Dandelion Launchers, Stage 8.

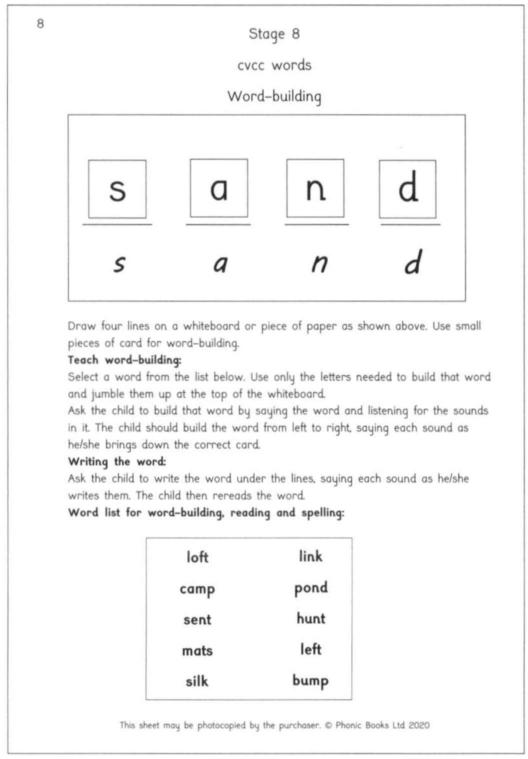

8

Stage 8

cvcc words

Word-building

s a n d

s a n d

Draw four lines on a whiteboard or piece of paper as shown above. Use small pieces of card for word-building.

Teach word-building:

Select a word from the list below. Use only the letters needed to build that word and jumble them up at the top of the whiteboard.

Ask the child to build that word by saying the word and listening for the sounds in it. The child should build the word from left to right, saying each sound as he/she brings down the correct card.

Writing the word:

Ask the child to write the word under the lines, saying each sound as he/she writes them. The child then rereads the word.

Word list for word-building, reading and spelling:

loft	link
camp	pond
sent	hunt
mats	left
silk	bump

This sheet may be photocopied by the purchaser. © Phonic Books Ltd 2020

This activity involves using a whiteboard or paper with lines drawn underneath each sound. Small card pieces are used to construct words. The activity starts by the teacher selecting a word from a specified list, then jumbling its letters at the top of the whiteboard. The student then builds the word by articulating and identifying the sounds, arranging the cards from left to right. Each sound is emphasized as the corresponding card is placed. Afterwards, the student writes the word below the lines, saying each sound during the writing process.

Three blending methods

Blending is a pivotal skill in learning to read, where students combine individual sounds (phonemes) to form whole words. Here are three distinct methods designed to enhance a student's ability to decode and blend words. Each method offers a unique approach to breaking down words into sounds and merging them to form complete words.

Method 1: Decode and blend

"Say the sounds and read the word."

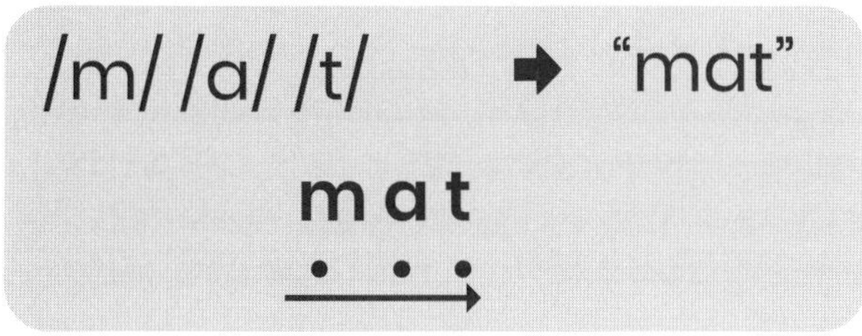

The student points to and says the sounds in the word one at a time, pointing to each sound. Then they move their finger under the whole word, blending all the sounds into the word. This first method has a greater load on working memory relative to the next two methods.

Method 2: Stretch and blend

"Stretch the sounds and push them together to read the word."

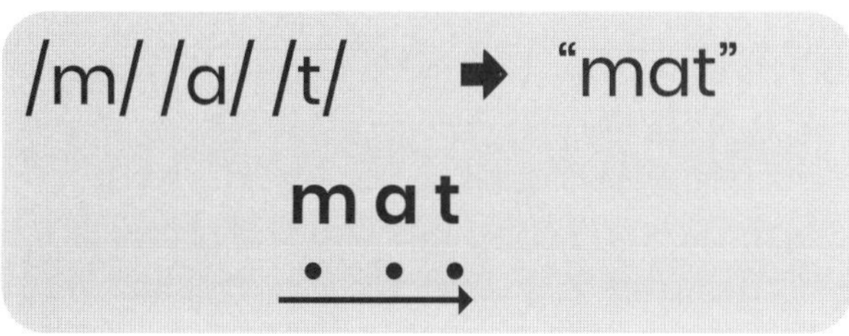

The teacher points to the first letter/sound, asking the student to say the sound and stretch it until their finger reaches the next sound in the word. The teacher moves their finger under the whole word, as the student blends all the sounds in the word.

Method 3: Blend and add

"Blend the first two sounds, then add the next sound."

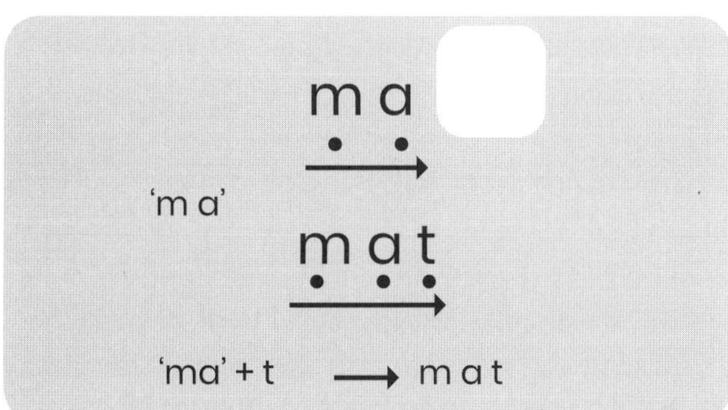

The teacher conceals the third letter/sound. Next, the teacher moves their finger under the first two sounds and asks the learner to blend just two sounds, e.g. 'm' + 'a' = 'ma.' Then the teacher repeats 'ma.' The teacher reveals the last letter/sound and asks the student to add 't.' Finally, the teacher points under the whole word as the student reads "mat."

Methods 2 and 3 have a lesser load on working memory relative to the first method.

How to write a word chain

A **word chain** is a list of words used to develop phonemic awareness skills: blending, segmenting, and phoneme manipulation. These are the underlying skills needed for reading. Word-chain activities are the most effective way to develop these skills.

In a word-chain activity, the teacher will ask the student to build a word (with letter cards or letters) and read it. The student is then asked to make a change to the word; for example, "Change the word 'pot' to 'pit'." The student will need to identify where the change in the word has occurred and then change, remove, or add the letter needed to read the new word.

What does a word chain look like?

This is an example of a word chain:

Letters: s, a, t, i, m, n, o, p

Word chain: nip—nap—tap—top—mop—map—sap—sip—tip

Many programs include word-chain activities, but it is useful to know how to write one. This skill allows the teacher to design a word-chain activity that can address a specific difficulty a student may have. For example, the student may confuse the sound and spelling of /ch/ and /sh/. A word chain to address this difficulty would look like this:

> **Letters: m, u, sh, ch, n, b, f, i, p, a, r, c**
> **Word chain:** mush—much—munch—bunch—bun—shun—shin—fin—finch—inch—pinch—pin—bin—ban—bash—brash—brush—crush—crash

The two examples above use real words, and this is suitable for young students. For older students, you can also use nonsense word chains. A typical example would look like this:

> **Letters: b, l, i, n, a, o, t, u**
> **Word chain:** blin—blan—lan—lon—lont—lunt—lut—blut

Here are some guidelines for creating a word chain:

1. Use one syllable words.
2. Use spellings from the simple code. It can get very confusing if vowel teams are included as many of them can be pronounced in different ways.
3. The word chain can include changing sounds, removing sounds, and adding sounds.
4. Make only one change at a time.

How to teach reading

One of the primary goals in teaching phonics is to equip students with the skills necessary to decode and comprehend text effectively. When students are reading, encourage them to sound out each word phonetically and then blend these sounds to form words. This lays the groundwork for developing fluent reading skills, as it enables students to approach unfamiliar words with confidence. Slow, laboured reading can interfere with comprehension. When a student reads very slowly, reread each sentence after them to maintain comprehension of the text.

Once students are comfortable with sounding out and blending words, a next step could be to read a book from a previous lesson for a second time or multiple times to enhance fluency. This repetition helps to consolidate students' decoding skills. As students revisit the text, they begin to transition from mechanical decoding to reading with greater fluency.

This can be progressed to teaching them to vary their pitch, pace, and emphasis according to the words and punctuation in the text. Reading with expression not only makes the reading experience more fun but also aids in comprehension, as it brings the text to life and highlights its meaning.

How to correct reading errors

One of the most important elements of learning is receiving error feedback. With every error feedback, the student can adjust their knowledge or skill and can fine-tune them and make their reading increasingly accurate. Making and correcting errors is a great learning opportunity!

Reading with our students is a fantastic opportunity for error feedback. But before we can address the error, we need to know what kind of error the reader is making. Here are a few tips:

1. Error feedback should be a positive experience in which the student can succeed. So, after the feedback has taken place, the student should be able

to use the new information and read a word or sentence successfully.

2. It is very helpful to use a pointer or a pencil to show the student where the error occurred in the word. The error can even occur between letters on the page, so accurate pointing is essential.
3. When the student has read the word correctly, it is helpful to reread the whole sentence so that they can reread the correct word in the context of the text.

What kinds of reading errors do students make?

Lack of Alphabetic Code knowledge

Many students make reading errors because they have insufficient knowledge of the Alphabetic Code. For example, when a student reads the word "goat" as /g/ /o/ /a/ /t/, we can see that they don't know that the grapheme 'oa' spells the sound /oe/.

So, how can feedback be given? Point to both letters and say: "These two letters represent one sound: /oe/. Sound out the word with /oe/ here (pointing to the letters 'oa')." The student then blends the sounds together: /g/ /oe/ /t/ → "goat."

Not matching sounds to graphemes (letter/s)

Students may add or omit sounds when they read. To develop reading accuracy, they will need to match the graphemes to the sounds in the word. Here are typical examples of reading errors.

Adding sounds: When a student reads the word "back" as "black," we can see that they are adding the sound /l/. To give feedback, point to the word and say: "You read "black" but there is no /l/ here (pointing to the place the 'l' would be in the word "black"). Sound out the word." The student should then sound the word correctly: /b/ /a/ /k/ → "back."

Omitting sounds: When a student reads the word "frog" as "fog," we can see that they are omitting a sound in the word. To give feedback, point to the letter 'r' and say: "There is a /r/ here. Sound out the word with the /r/ here (pointing to the letter 'r')." The student then sounds out the word pointing to the letters /f/ /r/ /o/ /g/ → "frog."

Reversing a word

When a student reads "was" for "saw," we can see that they have flipped the word. So, how can feedback be given? Ask the student to sound out the word. /s/ /aw/. Remind the student that 'aw' spells /aw/. Ask the student to blend the sounds into a word: /s/ /aw/ → "saw."

Developing vocabulary

Systematic synthetic phonics focuses on the mechanics of learning to read: developing the skills to sound out, blend to read, and segment to spell. It is a structured, progressive program towards reading fluency. However, alongside that process, it's critical to develop the broader reading skills: prosody, pace, comprehension, and vocabulary. Phonics success is based on careful, steady progression, so that students are only exposed to words in their books which contain the sounds and high-frequency words they know. Yet, every reading experience is an opportunity to develop a student's wider vocabulary, through questioning and discussion. For example: books within the Dandelion World Series include nonfiction Knowledge Builder pages intended for children and adults to read together, which help to reinforce vocabulary and enhance comprehension skills, by encouraging the student to think about what they have read.

Talking about the words students decode: exploring meaning, looking at patterns, and discussing synonyms and antonyms will not only help secure comprehension and reading for meaning, but will also grow and develop a student's more general language knowledge. For example, while reading the word "swift," students can explore synonyms like "quick" and "fast," and antonyms such as "slow." Discussing these words not only enhances vocabulary but also clarifies the concept of speed as it applies to different contexts, thereby enhancing students' understanding of linguistic relationships.

Oracy is one of the key elements of vocabulary development; therefore, alongside the phonics skills, high-quality discussion around texts furthers the learning opportunities and outcomes.

There are lots of different ways to structure the discussion and get the most out of every page in a reading book—at any level.

For instance, in Book 3a: Sam's Bag (Dandelion Launchers), the following prompts could be used around pages 3 and 4 in order to extend the language around the book.

- What words rhyme with "bag"? (tag, sag, rag, nag)
- Where is Tam? (at the bus stop)
- Who else is in the picture? (Sam)
- What might you put in a bag? (pens and pencils, books, water bottle, lunchbox)

- What can you see on the bag? (a name tag)
- Whose name is on the tag? (Tam)
- How do you think Tam feels? (happy, excited, pleased)

Likewise, at a phonetically more challenging level there are still plenty of discursive opportunities, for example in Book 15a: Ding Dong (Dandelion Launchers) the following prompts could be used around the content on pages 5–6:

- What is another word for "ding"? (dong, chime, ring)
- What makes sounds like "ding" and "dong"? (bells, doorbells)
- What doex the expression "fed up" mean? (tired, annoyed, frustrated)
- Why do you think Tam is feeling "fed up"? (She is tired of having to get up and go to the door every time the doorbell ring.)
- How do you think Tam will feel if the doorbell stops ringing? (relieved, peaceful, relaxed, or still annoyed)

How to teach reading comprehension

For students to become fluent readers, they need to be able to understand what they are reading. Students should be encouraged to discuss what happens in the stories and to give spoken answers to comprehension questions. This improves student's understanding of language, develops their wider vocabulary and increases their interest in learning to read.

The activity books contain various types of activities to enable students to put their comprehension skills into practice. For example, Dandelion Launchers Stages 1–7 Activities includes **Retelling the story** activities where students retell the story or create their own story using the pictures and word cards provided on tho page.

Other comprehension activities include matching words to the correct pictures from the story, or this **Make a book** activity where students read the text and then draw a picture to match the text on each page.

As the program progresses, more activities are introduced, with increasing emphasis on reading comprehension. For instance, in the VCe Spellings Activities, the **What happens next?** activity is introduced.

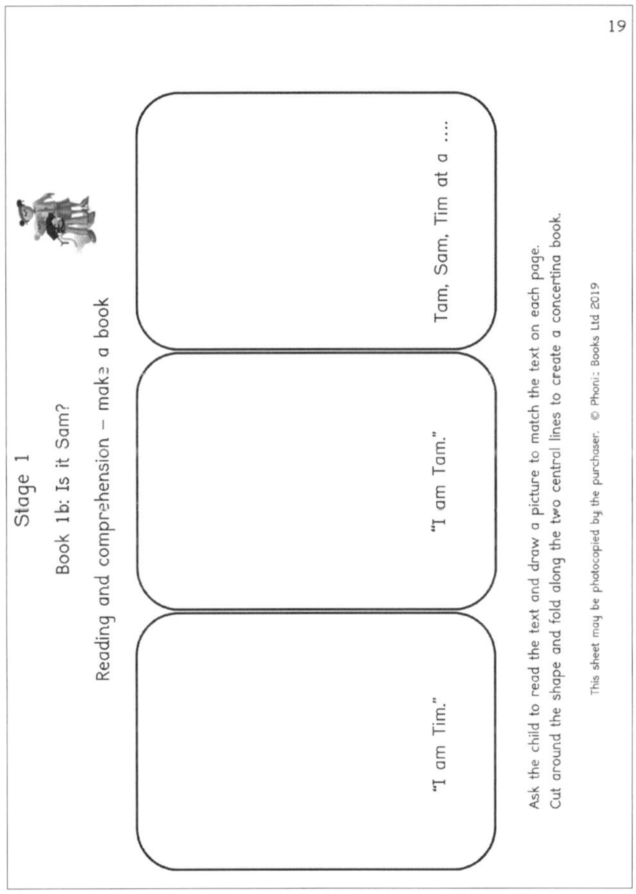
19

Stage 1

Book 1b: Is it Sam?

Reading and comprehension – make a book

"I am Tim."

"I am Tam."

Tam, Sam, Tim at a ....

Ask the child to read the text and draw a picture to match the text on each page.
Cut around the shape and fold along the two central lines to create a concertina book.

This sheet may be photocopied by the purchaser. © Phonic Books Ltd 2019

16

Stage 1

Book 1a: Sam, Tam, Tim

Retelling the story

Sit, Tam.

Tim Tam Sam

sit sat

This page can be photocopied onto card. Cut out these pictures for retelling the story or for children to make their own story. Picture cards are arranged in story order. Choose whether to number them on the back. Word cards can also be used to reinforce vocabulary.

This sheet may be photocopied by the purchaser. © Phonic Books Ltd 2019

Here, students are presented with a passage from a story and are invited to underline their favorite part, followed by creating a drawing that corresponds to the narrative. Additionally, the **Find the untruths** activity challenges students with a story passage containing deliberate errors. Their task is to identify these mistakes, helping to develop their attention to detail and comprehension skills.

How to change bad guessing habits?

Many students will have been encouraged to use guessing strategies, such as guessing clues from the picture or the context, and/or skipping the word and reading to the end of the sentence to guess what a word might be. Despite research indicating the limited effectiveness of these strategies, they continue to be widely adopted in educational settings.

Guessing strategies may seem to help students reading a very simple, repetitive text; however, they let students down once the pictures fall away. Guessing leads to inaccurate reading, which affects comprehension. The clues for decoding a word are in the letters on the page and that is where students need to focus their attention.

Many older readers have bad guessing habits that are difficult to undo. One of the ways we can try and change these deeply ingrained habits is to reward the student when they demonstrate decoding. This can be in the shape of counters that the student accumulates as they work out the words by sounding them out.

A popular game is the "chest of gold." The game involves students earning yellow counters as they decode their way through a text. If the student resorts to guessing, the teacher gets the gold from the chest. This game can help the student to focus on the task at hand.

How to teach letter formation

Following reading and comprehension activities, the next step is to teach students how to practice writing the graphemes they have learned.

First, learning how to grip a pencil correctly is an important step for developing neat handwriting. The pencil should rest comfortably between the thumb and index finger, supported by the middle finger, with the other two fingers curled inwards. With their hands resting on the table, students should learn to move the pencil forward using their hand muscles. Regular practice in letter formation and careful monitoring of each student's technique during dictation exercises are key to cultivating long-term neat handwriting and preventing the development of poor habits.

When teaching letter formation, it is recommended to use lined paper that will demonstrate the proportions of ascender and descender letters. This way the students can practice forming letters correctly from the get go.

Teachers play a vital role in this learning process. They can demonstrate letter formation effectively by writing on the whiteboard or visually tracing the letters' movements in the air.

Book 2: Pete 37

Find the untruths

Reading comprehension

The kitchen was a mess. Dad made Steve, the robot. The robot dropped the trash on Mom's bed. The glass smashed. He cracked the sink in the kitchen. Mom had to press 'delete' to stop him. Mom had to do the dishes.

There are **5** untruths in this story. Can you spot them?

Ask the student to read the text carefully and underline any 'untruth' that has been planted in the story.

This sheet may be photocopied by the purchaser. © Phonic Books Ltd 2021

How to teach spelling

The activity books offer a variety of exercises to practice spelling, such as **Fill in the missing sounds**, where students are given incomplete words for them to fill in with the correct letter for the missing sound. To reinforce their learning, students should be encouraged to vocalize the sounds as they write, and then blend these sounds together while forming each word.

They also include activities, such as **Fill in all the missing sounds**, where students fill in every letter for all the missing sounds in the words they've just practiced in the preceding activity.

Finally, as students to progress towards more autonomous writing, the activity books also include **Sentence dictation** activities. These activities are accompanied by illustrative pictures, offering visual context to aid in comprehension. Students are encouraged to phonetically sound out the words as they spell them, reinforcing their understanding of the relationship between sounds and spelling.

Stage 2 29

New sounds: n o p

Fill in the missing sounds

P _ m | _ a n | m a _

c _ p | p _ n | P _ p

Fill in the missing sounds to complete the words. Encourage the child to say the sounds as they write them and then blend the three sounds in each word together to read the word.

This sheet may be photocopied by the purchaser. © Phonic Books Ltd 2019

How to do a dictation activity

Dictation is a great way to consolidate the bonds between reading and spelling. It is a controlled exercise where students can succeed because the teacher includes words with spellings the students have already learned. Unlike a story writing activity where the students will attempt to spell words they may not be able to encode yet, dictation provides a "safe" activity where all students can succeed.

Dictation can be done at word level or sentence level. Writing and spelling words is hugely taxing on working memory. The student must hear and understand the word or sentence. Then, they must hold it in working memory while retrieving a letter/s (grapheme) for each sound in each word. Some students may forget the word or part of the sentence. For this reason, it is important to follow a clear routine for dictation.

Dictation activities can serve as useful records of learning and identifying difficulties that students are experiencing. It can be done on small individual whiteboards or in notebooks. The teacher can photograph or keep these and identify any students who need further support.

Many students will still have difficulties forming letters correctly. The purpose of a dictation activity is to see how students use their phonics knowledge to encode words. If the words are illegible, letter formation should be addressed. If not, find another opportunity to work on letter formation.

14

Stage 1

Book 1a: Sam, Tam, Tim

Sentence dictation

"I __ ___."

___ ___.

Cut or fold the sheet along the dotted line above before offering to the child. Offer the sentences below as dictation. Encourage the child to sound out the words as they spell them.

1. "I am Sam." 2. Sam sat.

This sheet may be photocopied by the purchaser. © Phonic Books Ltd 2019

Single word dictation

Choose a list of words that the students have been learning. Make sure they have had sufficient practice reading and spelling these words. Say the word first; next, put it within the context of a sentence; and then repeat the word. This way the students can understand the word before they write it down. Pause after each word to check that all the students have finished writing.

The teacher can say, for example:

> "I am going to dictate some words and I would like you to write them down.
> dog. The dog barked. dog.
> bag. Gran has a bag. bag.
> gap. There is a gap in the road. gap."
> etc.

Sentence dictation

Writing a sentence is more taxing on working memory than remembering one word at a time and spelling it. Some students will find it difficult to hold the complete sentence in working memory. It is good practice to break any long sentences into parts to enable all students to keep up. After all, we are not checking working memory but how students represent the words with graphemes they have learned.

The teacher will need to decide if they provide their students with high-frequency words that have more complex spellings, for example "the." These words can be written on the board to remind the students how to spell them.

The teacher will also need to decide whether they will include capital letters and periods in this activity. This depends on whether this has been taught previously.

Dictated sentences will need to be decodable—this means that all the words, except a few necessary high-frequency words, will be within the knowledge of the students. The teacher can write these sentences or take them from a decodable book the students have read. For beginner readers, just one or two sentences will be sufficient for this activity.

The teacher can say:
"I am going to dictate a sentence.
I would like you to listen to it and then say it.
Then, write it down.
'Bob got on the top.'"

The teacher repeats:
"'Bob got on the top.' Now you say it."
Students repeat:
"'Bob got on the top.'"
Students write the sentence.

Bob got on the top.

2

How to teach high-frequency words

High-frequency words are frequently used words that can potentially present a challenge to students: they cannot easily read or write them through decoding, such as blending and listening for sounds. This difficulty arises because these words often contain letter–sound combinations that the students have not yet learned.

The program gradually introduces high-frequency words to expand the students' vocabulary. The scheme of work charts, found on page 28, list all the high-frequency words introduced in each book covered by the lesson plans in this manual. Furthermore, each Reader conveniently lists the high-frequency words featured in its story at the beginning of the book, providing an easy reference for both students and teachers.

The chart on pages 45–46 provides the first 300 high-frequency words taught in the program.

THE FIRST 300 HIGH-FREQUENCY WORDS

Simple spellings

vc
am
an
at
if
in
it
on
up
us

/ck/
ba**ck**
bla**ck**
du**ck**

v
a

vcc
and
end
its

cvc /a/
b**a**t
c**a**n
c**a**t
r**a**n
d**a**d
h**a**d
m**a**n
s**a**t

cvcc
best
fast
help
just
jump
land
left
last
list
milk
must
nest
next
went

cvc /e/
b**e**d
g**e**t
l**e**t
m**e**n
b**e**ll
r**e**d
s**e**t
t**e**n
w**e**ll
y**e**s

ccvc
from
still
spot
stop
gran
step

cvc /i/
b**i**g
d**i**d
h**i**m
s**i**t
s**i**x
m**i**ss

/th/ (voiced)
that
the
them
then
this
wi**th**

/th/ (unvoiced)
think

cvc /o/
b**o**x
d**o**g
g**o**t
h**o**t
m**o**m
n**o**t

/w/
when
which

/sh/
fi**sh**
wi**sh**

/ch/
mu**ch**
su**ch**

cvc /u/
b**u**t
c**u**t
f**u**n
r**u**n

/z/
a**s**
i**s**
ha**s**
hi**s**

/ng/
alo**ng**
bri**ng**
ki**ng**
lo**ng**
so**ng**
thi**ng**

/v/
gi**ve**
ha**ve**
li**ve**
o**f**

THE FIRST 300 HIGH-FREQUENCY WORDS

Complex spellings

/ae/
cake
came
gave
late
made
make
name
take
day
may
play
say
way
always
away
great
eight
they

/e/
again
said
head
read
bread
any
many
friends

/oe/
go
going
no
so
both
cold
don't
old
hold
told
most
only
open
boat
coat
home
those
grow
know
own
show
though

/ie/
I
child
find
kind
five
like
line
time
white
write
by
my
fly
try
why
high
night
right

/i/
been

/ee/
be
he
me
she
we
even
these
feel
feet
green
keep
need
see
sleep
tree
three
each
eat
leave
tea
please
read
baby
carry
every
really
very
key

/or/
or
door
floor
corn
for
horse
morning
before
more
short

/oi/
boy
toy

/ow/
about
around
found
house
mouse
out
our
round
ground
down
cow
how
now
town

Uncommon spellings
one
once
two
people
everyone

/er/
her
after
better
ever
father
letter
never
over
paper
river
under
water
were
birds
first
girl
picture
work

/oo/
moon
do
to
into
who
together
cool
food
school
soon
too
group
new

Multisyllable words
American
children
different
little
magic
rabbit
suddenly

/aw/
all
fall
ball
call
small
walk
talk
saw

/ar/
are
car
dark
far
farm
hard
garden
park
start

/air/
air
bear
their
there
where

/u/
mother
does
come
some
was

/o/
what
want
watch

/oo/
look
book
good
look
took
wood
put
could
would

/ue/
use

How to teach vocabulary when reading a decodable book

Decodable books often include target words that students may not know. There are many reasons why students may not know words in a text:

- The word may be unusual.
- The students may have limited language as English language learners.
- The students may have a language disability.
- The students may have had limited opportunities to read books at home.

Learning new vocabulary is beneficial for all students. It helps them develop their expressive and receptive language. This will also develop their comprehension as they become readers.

When we teach new vocabulary, we want our students to learn how a word sounds and how it is spelled. We want them to make connections to words they already know, so the new vocabulary is stored securely in long-term memory and can be retrieved when needed.

Here is how we recommend teaching students new words encountered in a decodable book. The example here is the word "chest" from Book 11a: Nuts for Lunch from the Dandelion Launchers series.

1. Demonstrate how letters map onto the sounds in the word.

chest	or	ch	e	s	t

2. Say the word clearly. Ask the students to repeat the word. All too often students are not confident in pronouncing new words. /ch/ /e/ /s/ /t/ → "chest." This is particularly important when the word has more than one syllable as students need to know which syllable to stress.
3. Define the word. For example, "The word 'chest' means a big, strong box that you can store things in. Or it can mean the part of your body between your neck and stomach." (A simple definition can often be found in the decodable book.)
4. Give an example from the decodable book. Ask questions, such as, "What is the chest being used for?" Students can answer in their own words ("to store nuts").

Stan had a chest.
It was next to the bench.

1

5. Keep the word on the board and revisit throughout the week.

How to read a nonfiction decodable book

While the main lesson plans in this teacher manual predominantly focus on Dandelion Launchers, which is centred around fiction, this section delves into nonfiction decoding. This is particularly relevant for teachers who would like to incorporate resources from the Dandelion World series, a nonfiction parallel series to the Dandelion Launchers.

Nonfiction decodable books are wonderful reading resources. They combine two essential parts of reading: word recognition (decoding) and world knowledge (language comprehension and subject vocabulary).

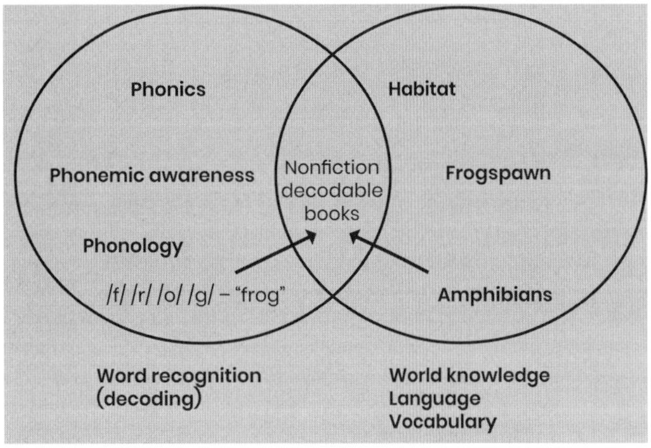

Educators now recognize that world knowledge has an important part to play in reading comprehension. Students who lack world knowledge can't make sense of a text that presumes they have general knowledge. For example, a sentence that describes a character as a "fossil" will have little meaning to a student who has not learned about what fossils are and how they are created.

The Dandelion World series features "Knowledge Builder" pages that include pictures and text about the subject of the book. The series also includes a glossary so that students can learn new words that are beyond their decoding skills. By including knowledge-building pages, which are intended for student to read with an adult, the students can develop their world knowledge orally without being limited only to a text they can read. As learning about a subject supports reading comprehension, it is advisable to immerse the students in the knowledge first and only then read the decodable book.

Before reading the decodable text, teachers can start by asking the students what they know about the topic. This way new learning is built on what the students already understand and know. Then teachers can read the "Knowledge Builder" pages to the students and teach the vocabulary. Next, they can then ask questions to ensure that the students have understood the subject and vocabulary. They then read the decodable books and facilitate a discussion. Finally, teachers can link the text the students have decoded to the subject knowledge already learned.

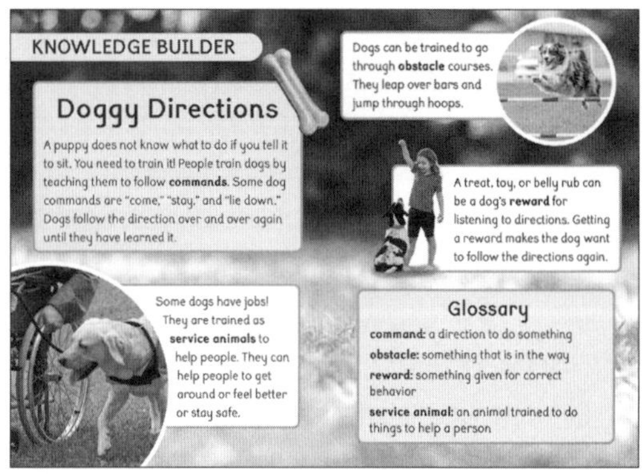
KNOWLEDGE BUILDER

Doggy Directions

A puppy does not know what to do if you tell it to sit. You need to train it! People train dogs by teaching them to follow **commands**. Some dog commands are "come," "stay," and "lie down." Dogs follow the direction over and over again until they have learned it.

Dogs can be trained to go through **obstacle** courses. They leap over bars and jump through hoops.

A treat, toy, or belly rub can be a dog's **reward** for listening to directions. Getting a reward makes the dog want to follow the directions again.

Some dogs have jobs! They are trained as **service animals** to help people. They can help people to get around or feel better or stay safe.

Glossary

command: a direction to do something
obstacle: something that is in the way
reward: something given for correct behavior
service animal: an animal trained to do things to help a person

FLUENCY AND PROSODY

Fluency in reading encompasses the ability to read text accurately and quickly but also with proper expression, known as prosody. Each of these elements are integral for constructing meaning. Fluency and comprehension are interlinked; disfluent reading can significantly hinder comprehension, while difficulty with comprehension can in turn impede fluency. Therefore, the development of a reading pace that supports comprehension, alongside accurate and expressive reading of all words—including high-frequency words—is a fundamental aspect of learning to read.

If students are not able to read fluently, it is a useful indicator of where revision and consolidation are required. Specific grapheme–phoneme correspondences or high-frequency words can be targeted and upskilled to increase a student's confidence.

Once students are reading evenly and quickly, with no overt blending, and correctly differentiating between the individual words, it is useful to re-read the text with prosody in mind (reading rhythmically, with intonation and expression).

The basics of sound grapheme–phoneme correspondence knowledge and secure blending skills need to be in place before fluency and prosody can be achieved, but working on these simultaneously, with each text read multiple times, will ensure a more rounded, successful reading experience with much better comprehension outcomes. When students are focusing on the mechanics of decoding, they are far less likely to grasp meaning from the text than when they read quicker, with no audible blending and with a tone that reflects the content. Reading success and enjoyment is dependent on decoding competence *and* fluent, expressive pace, but it's easy for the latter to get forgotten in the race to achieve decoding proficiency.

A large part of reading accurately and with expression is about understanding punctuation and what impact it has on the text. Encouraging students from the very start of their reading journey to "read" commas and full stops, to change their tone at the beginning and end of a sentence, for parentheses, for speech, and to draw breath at the right points is critical for effective prosody.

In texts as early as Book 1a: Sam, Tam, Tim (Dandelion Launchers), the language features signify the tone. For example: the repetition of "Sam sat." and "Tim sat." influences the intonation and encourages a particular rhythm. In Book 2a: Pam (Dandelion Launchers), "Pam is on the pot" might be read slightly louder, with more emphasis and enthusiasm, perhaps with a smile to mirror the humorous illustration and help convey meaning.

It can be useful to model reading the text in different ways, with and without expression, in order to highlight the contrast and demonstrate how much meaning can be grasped by the *way* words are read, not just by the words themselves. Understanding how to interpret literary techniques, such as repetition (for example, as an indication of emphasis) will enhance what students get out of text, but it will also help develop what they put into their own texts, with meaningful, sophisticated writing skills.

As the text complexity develops, so does the opportunity for prosody. For example, in Book 15a: Ding! Dong! (Dandelion Launchers), there is a significant amount of direct speech where expression is crucial, such as on page 2: "'Can I have an egg?' Tam brings Sam an egg." Students should practice reading this in a polite and expectant tone for Sam.

On page 4, the repetition of the request: "'Can I have a bit of milk?' Tam brings Tim the milk," provides another opportunity for varied expression.

Page 5 introduces a change in Tam's emotions: "Ding, dong! Ding, dong! The bell rings. Tam is fed up." This sudden shift in Tam's mood should be read with a tone of frustration, reflecting Tam's growing annoyance with the constant demands.

Finally, on page 6: "Tim and Sam sing Tam a song," the tone should shift to one of gratitude or joy. The singing can be read in a cheerful and melodic tone to convey the relief and happiness of the moment.

As the emotional descriptions change, so too should the tone and expression of the reader. When characters move from making polite requests (pages 2 and 4) to feeling a sense of frustration (page 5) and finally to expressing gratitude and joy (page 6), the use of direct speech and varied actions requires different vocal tones. This variation in tone and expression helps bring the story to life and engages the reader emotionally.

As the text reveals more of the emotion—through a greater array of punctuation, direct speech, and more sophisticated description, there is less reliance on the illustrations. However, as with earlier texts, they can be used to build into the prosody and to further enhance the meaning that children make.

The objective of reading with prosody (in addition to accuracy) is that children move away from the mechanical, unnatural pattern of decoding, developed in the early stages of phonics learning, to a rhythmic, expressive style that shows an understanding of what the writer intended them to think and feel about a text.

DIFFERENTIATION

Because of the nature of phonics teaching (the fast, systematic pace), the ideal is to keep the class or cohort together, progressing together. However, this relies on the pace of students' learning needs being similar, which isn't always the case, and there are many reasons why some students will struggle with different aspects of phonics learning. Maintaining a clear picture of how individuals are coping with the new skills as they are taught means that needs can be identified the moment they become apparent, ensuring that no student gets left behind. Those needs can then be met through a range of activities (delivered in a variety of formats) to bolster and fill any skill gaps, so that students can keep up with their peers and continue their learning with the rest of the group.

It is important to recognize the level of need in terms of whether students are some way off expectations, or just below them, so that the right support can be provided. In the most part, those not meeting expectations would benefit from small-group work to target and consolidate shared skill challenges before they become significant issues. However, the students who are significantly behind expectations (e.g. within the lowest-achieving 20%) are likely to benefit from more specialized, bespoke, individual intervention delivered one-to-one.

The Phonic Books program has a huge volume of resources to accompany every reading book to practice and consolidate learning at each point in the journey. Therefore, when a couple or small group of students are identified as struggling with the same concept, such as a specific grapheme–phoneme correspondence or particular high-frequency words, small-group work using or adapting the activities provided enables a useful, collaborative environment to reinforce learning and upskill the area of challenge.

For example, if students are struggling with any of the grapheme–phoneme correspondences or with blending specifics, during their reading of Dandelion Launchers Book 2a: Pam, there is a wealth of material to support them:

- Depending on which grapheme–phoneme correspondences are proving a struggle, the **Sound cards** and **Word-building cards** from Book 1a: Sam, Tam, Tim, Book 1b: Is it Sam?, and Book 2a: Pam (all in the accompanying activity book), could be revisited. To avoid these being used in the same way as the main lesson and feeling repetitive or predictable, there are lots of creative ways that they can be manipulated (see the next section).
- Re-playing some of the games, e.g. the (bingo **Game** from the readers, or the **Dice game** from the accompanying activity book) provides the opportunity for repeated practice.

It is also possible that students will be secure in the sounds but have trouble making meaning from the text. This is often due to the cognitive load of decoding. For these obstacles, a different focus would be beneficial, again using the material provided. For example: students could work one-to-one, in pairs, or in small groups to retell or recap the story, using the pictures, words, and sentence matching (in the activity book). The ability to accurately and coherently sequence events is critical in early reading comprehension.

As students progress through the program, and the phonics becomes more complex, the volume, range, and variety of accompanying activities increases, providing plenty of differentiation opportunities. For example, in Dandelion Readers Set 1: The Paddle, if students find the sound for the 'le' spelling challenging, the following material could be utilised in various different formats:

- The grapheme cards from the accompanying activity books, and the Reading practice pages within the readers, would provide an opportunity for revision and reinforcement. Again, the next section provides some creative ideas for differentiation at this level.
- Revisiting the games, for example the **4-in-a-row**, **Stepping stones**, and memory games, also provides useful and fun opportunities for consolidation.

If the stumbling block is around comprehension at a higher level, some vocabulary work would be useful to ensure students understand the words they're decoding. Activities that support this include:

- Looking at real and nonsense 'le' words (from the activity book) is beneficial, particularly if students are asked for definitions as they go.
- Matching sentences to pictures (from the activity book) supports sequencing and plot recapping; these activities can all be executed orally, in writing or in a more dynamic, physical capacity such as through role play or mime.
- Using these resources, as well as any of the images from the readers can also help drill down further into the text depth, if discussion is promoted; supporting students to explore how characters feel and think enables much more robust comprehension to be reached.

It is useful to have a flexible approach to differentiation, and to be aware that students are likely to move in and out of different small groups and sometimes not need additional support at all. The idea is that the groups flex and change according to the needs of the class, to ensure continual, steady progress for all students.

English as an additional or foreign language

For students joining the cohort late, and those with English as an additional language, the key is on-entry assessment to see how much phonic knowledge has already been acquired. This means that students start at the right point in the program, whatever their prior experience. Because of the methodical, rigorous nature of systematic synthetic phonics teaching, the pedagogy is very inclusive. However, it's important to be aware of existing concepts of language for those with English as an additional language, which may make grasping the fundamentals (specifically the grapheme–phoneme correspondences) more challenging than for native English-speaking kindergarten students. Having said that, students with English as an additional language are likely to catch up quickly with their peers, and so need fast-paced, short-term differentiated tuition, and then not need ongoing additional support, at least not on a phonic level. It's more likely that the stumbling blocks for students with English as an additional language will be around comprehension, for which any of the strategies identified here can be applied. Additionally, it's worth considering extra pronunciation support (to also be available at home for parental use).

Strategies for phonics differentiation

Any of these creative ideas can be adapted according to specific grapheme–phoneme correspondences and/or high-frequency words. They all work to practice and consolidate the key phonic skills, as well as build confidence and familiarity more generally.

Grapheme–phoneme correspondence recognition

- Hold the sound cards behind your back and draw them out one at a time for students to practice sounding out. You can do this quicker and quicker as they become more confident, mixing up the order and increasing the pace. This works with high-frequency words, too.
- Stick the sound cards around the classroom (or playground) and ask students to hop to one sound, skip to one and jump to another as you call them out.
- Find a selection of items in the classroom that start with the sounds on the grapheme cards, and ask students to sort the items into different groups according to what sound they start with.
- Choose a sound from the cards and encourage students to go on a treasure hunt around the classroom to find as many things as they can that begin with that sound.

High-frequency words

- Play a card-matching game. Can the student find the matching card, for example, for the word "is"?

Blending

- Stick the sound cards on individual building blocks and encourage students to put the blocks together to "build" simple words. Say each sound together and then help students to blend them together to read the words out loud. Next, try separating the blocks again to segment the word back into its individual sounds.
- See the recommendations for how to teach blending (pages 36–37). Methods 2 and 3 can be particularly effective for students who are struggling. For Method 2 (Stretch and Blend), for example the word "mat," use a toy car or moving toy to stretch the sounds until the car moves to the next sound: /mmmmmaaaaat/. For Method 3 (Add and Blend), hide the last letter in the word. Using a toy car, ask the student to blend the first two sounds and move the car underneath the two first letters: 'ma.' Then add the third letter, and move the toy car under the three letters: 'ma' + 't' = "mat."
- Place all the sound cards on the table, and see how many different words students can build. They need to write the words they have built down.

ASSESSMENT

Continuous assessment

To ensure students are confident with the new sounds they have learned in each lesson plan, it's important to track their progress using quick, formative assessments.

For example, the Dandelion Launchers activity books contain **Bookmarks**, which feature words printed on them that incorporate the phonic skills covered in the lessons. Teachers can check students are comfortable using these words before moving on to the next stage in the books.

Additionally, **Reading certificates** are found at the back of the activity books.

22

Stage 8

cvcc words

Bookmark with words for reading and spelling

cvcc words

mend
hand
lump
bond
milk
went

We have been working on

cvcc words

Help your child practice these sounds and then practice reading the words on the bookmark. Encourage them to blend the sounds together as they read the words.

Have fun!

Use these words for reading and spelling. Check that the children are comfortable with building and reading these words before moving on to the next stage of books. This can be used as a bookmark. Teachers may choose to cut out the information box and stick it to the reverse of the bookmark if sending home.

This sheet may be photocopied by the purchaser. © Phonic Books Ltd 2020

26

Stage 8

cvcc words

Spelling assessment

1. gift
2. mend
3. sank
4. pond
5. bump
6. milk
7. sent
8. honk
9. must
10. limp
11. band
12. went

This list can be used as a spelling assessment at the end of Stage 8. When dictating a word, first say the word on its own. Next, say a sentence with the word in it (to put the word in the context of a sentence) and then repeat the word. This ensures that the child has heard the word correctly, e.g. "Tent. It was fun to sleep in the tent. Tent." Encourage the children to sound out the words while writing them.

This sheet may be photocopied by the purchaser. © Phonic Books Ltd 2020

24

Congratulations!

You have read the book **Junk**

Signed by

Date achieved

PhonicBooks

This sheet may be photocopied by the purchaser. © Phonic Books Ltd 2020

Spelling assessments are introduced from Stage 8. These assessments involve dictation exercises where a word is first said in isolation, then used within a sentence, and finally repeated. This method ensures clarity in hearing and understanding the word. For example, the word "tent" might be presented as, "Tent. It was fun to sleep in the tent. Tent." This approach also encourages phonetic spelling, helping to develop writing skills.

Games within the activity books can also serve as a useful assessment tool. They provide immediate feedback, which is crucial for learning. Students understand quickly what they did right or wrong and learn from it, promoting faster and more effective learning.

Reading assessments

The following assessments can be used to work alongside the lesson plans in this manual. They can be used to evaluate reading progress over time and to identify where further help or consolidation is needed.

The assessments will identify the following:

- knowledge of grapheme–phoneme correspondences
- ability to blend sounds together accurately to decode single words
- ability to decode a sequential text at the reader's decoding level
- ability to comprehend a sequential text at the reader's decoding level

When to assess?

The teacher will decide when to assess and at what level. We suggest there should be at least a week after new learning and reading the relevant book, before delivering an assessment at that level. The results will then show which areas need revisiting for further instruction and practice.

We recommend that a teacher assess readers after a stage or unit of work, for example:

- at the end of Stage 7 Dandelion Launchers
- at CVCC, CCVC, and CCVCC level at the end of Stage 10 Dandelion Launchers
- after consonant digraphs th, ch, sh, ck, and ng at the end of Stage 15 Dandelion Launchers.
- at the end of VCe Spellings

High-frequency words

Our Dandelion Launchers series list the high-frequency words which appear in our stories at the beginning of each book.

Words stop being high-frequency words once the relevant sound spellings have been taught, but these words are initially necessary to construct proper sentences even in the earliest books. There are high-frequency words in the assessments: words which appear in the text to be read. Provide the reader with help if needed before the reader reads the text. Point to the grapheme(s), the sound(s) of which the reader has not yet been taught and give the reader the sound(s). Then ask the reader to blend the sounds together and read the word.

Delivering the assessment

Print the reading sheets on cream paper. This will prevent the black print on white paper "glare" which affects some children when reading.

- We recommend you laminate the diagnostic reading sheets for multiple use.
- The teacher will determine how often the reader needs re-assessment. We have provided for two re-assessments on the scoring sheet.
- Three errors in the single words or the text are enough to warrant a re-test at a later date.
- Encourage the reader to have a positive attitude towards being tested, with an understanding that it is to demonstrate their progress with reading. The tester could say something positive to the reader such as:
  "Today we are going to see how well you are doing!"
- Make sure, during testing, that the reader cannot see what is being written.
- Sit opposite rather than next to the reader.
- Use the same notation for each assessment. This will save time and make it easier to compare test results.
- Use a different colored pen for each re-test. This will enable quick comparison of results with an earlier test.
- It is suggested that errors with high-frequency words should not be part of the three-error re-test.

Comprehension questions

Reading accuracy is important, with comprehension as the goal. Increased fluency speed helps with comprehension, but knowledge of vocabulary is also key.

Two to four comprehension questions have been provided with each test. Let the reader re-read the text, if required, to find the answer, as these assessments are not memory tests.

Writing

Reading and writing should always be taught hand in hand at these early stages, enabling students' writing and spelling to progress at the same pace as their reading.

Ensure students practice spelling alongside reading at each new level of learning.

Phonic Books' photocopiable activity books provide many activities for this purpose at each level for all our sets and book series.

Responses recommended on the teacher's record sheet as the reader reads

Reading response	**Explanation of response** (When the reader has made an error, always put a line through the word and write above what the reader has said.)	**Symbol on record sheet**	**Example**	**Scoring**
Correct word	If the reader says the sound accurately (with no /uh/ sound after a consonant sound) or reads the word accurately by sight, write a ✓ above the letter/word.	✓	✓ ✓ ✓ ✓ u k m b ✓ ✓ ✓ pat mat sat	The reader scores 1 point for each correct sound/ word
Don't know	If the reader's response is "I don't know" or there is no response, put a line through the word and write **DK** above it.	**DK**	**DK** ~~stamp~~	No score
Self-corrects	If the reader self-corrects, write a ✓ and **SC** above.	✓ **SC**	✓ **SC** catch	The reader scores 1 point as the word is correct.
Sounds out the word	If the reader sounds out and reads the word accurately, write a ✓ and **SO** above.	**SO**	✓ **SO** stamp	The reader scores 1 point as the word is correct.
Misses a word in the text	If the reader misses out a word in the text, put a line through the word and write **MW** above it.	**MW**	**MW** ~~drink~~	No score
Adds an /uh/ after a sound	If the reader adds an /uh/ after a consonant sound, either in the letter sounds test or when sounding a word out, write ✓ **UH** above.	**UH**	✓**UH** m ✓**UH** fan	1 point

Analysis of errors to be done after the assessment

Reading response	Explanation of response (When the reader has made an error, always put a line through the word and write above what the reader has said.)	Symbol on record sheet	Example	Scoring
Adds a sound	The reader added a sound: "pond" for "pod."	**AD**	**AD** pond ~~pod~~	No score
Omits a sound	The reader omitted a sound: "back" for "black."	**OM**	**OM** back ~~black~~	No score
Visual error	The reader made a visual error: "bat" for "pat."	**VE**	**VE** bat ~~pat~~	No score
Guesses the word	The reader guessed the word. Put a line through the word and write what was said above. Later decide why the error was made.	**GU**	**GU** house ~~home~~	No score
Blending error	The reader sounded out the phonemes correctly but blended incorrectly: /s/ /e/ /n/ /d/ "said."	**BL**	**BL** said ~~send~~	No score

Marking the assessment and adding up the scores

Letter sounds:

- After the assessment, write tally marks 'I' in the first column each time one of the special symbols (e.g. DK, SC, VE) is used on the record sheet. This will give you a profile of the reader's approach to saying the sounds.
- If a reader says /em/ for /m/ they do not score a point. Readers cannot blend sounds with letter names. Examples that show the problem are: 'eff' begins with /e/, 'c' begins with /s/, 'g' begins with /j/, 'h' with /ae/, 'w' with /d/...
- If a reader says /muh/ for /m/ they score a point, but the reader needs to be taught clipped sounds. By putting a 'UH' above the word, it will remind the assessor that clipped sounds need to be taught to that reader going forward, as this will help increase fluency and eventually, when automaticity sets in, speed of reading.

- If the reader says the wrong sound, put a line through the sound, and write what was said above. Do not correct the reader.
- If the reader does not recognize the capital letters, carry on with the test, putting a line through the letter, and DK above.
- If the reader does not know the lower-case sounds, or makes at least one error, stop the test after finishing saying the sounds, as further work on phoneme–grapheme correspondence at this level is needed.
- Add up the points and write the score in the second column.

Single words

- After the assessment, write tally marks 'l' in the first column each time one of the special symbols (e.g. DK, SC, VE) is used on the record sheet. This will give you a profile of the reader's approach to reading single words.
- These words provide practice for the new sounds in the Stage being assessed as well as incorporating sounds from previous Stages. Score one point for each word read accurately, whether or not the word was sounded out or self-corrected.
- If the word was sounded out, put SO above the word. If there was self-correction, put SC above the word. These are not errors. By using these notations, the assessor will gain an understanding of the level of fluency the reader is operating at.
- BL indicates a blending difficulty. The reader will need more practice with this.
- OM and AD (omitting and adding sounds) point to poor blending skills. VE, which is a visual error, could be due to a specific developmental visual delay which could rectify itself over time. It might be a good idea to have the reader's vision checked. The same would apply if a reader misses a line when reading text, or MW, misses a word whilst reading the text. Notes about this can be put in the "Comments" box.
- Add up the points and write the score in the second column.

High-frequency words

Each school will have its own high-frequency word policy. Our books use a variety of these, listed at the front of each reading book. We are not testing high-frequency words in this test, so we do not score them in the overall score.

A minimum number of high-frequency words have been used in the reading texts and they are listed for practice before reading the text. (Stage 1 Assessment has only single words.)

Sequential text

- Write tally marks 'l' in the first column every time a special symbol is used on the record sheet. This will give you a profile of the reader's approach to reading text.
- Put any comments you may have in the "Comments" box below, for example, "Reader was put off by the amount of text," or "Reader needed a ruler under the line to help keep eyes on the lines of the text."
- To evaluate their decoding skills on the text, you may use the following formula for a percentage score:

  Score achieved ÷ Total score of test × 100
  = Percentage score

Comprehension

Comprehension is a very important part of the reading process. Early readers often concentrate hard on the decoding process, and do not take on board the sense of what they are reading. As automaticity sets in and reading becomes more fluent, they will start reading for meaning. For this reason, we recommend you allow them to re-read the text if necessary to answer the questions. The reading assessments are not a memory test.

Two to four comprehension questions are included for diagnostic purposes based on the reading text. Give one point for each question answered correctly. The assessor is to use their discretion as to the accuracy of the answer. Record your comments in the "Comments" box.

Final score

Add up the scores from the column on the right-hand side:

Sound score + Single word score + Text score + Comprehension score = Total score

Write the result in the Total score box at the bottom of the teacher's assessment record. If you wish to find a percentage score for the whole test, use the example formula below:

Score achieved ÷ Total score of test × 100
= Percentage score

$$32 \div 39 \times 100 = 82\%$$

Reading Assessment

Dandelion Series

ASSESSMENT FOR DANDELION LAUNCHERS: STAGES 1–7

1. Letter sounds (except q)
2. CVC words
3. Text at CVC, Stages 1–7

Response to reading: (For "record" write the appropriate code whilst testing; add the other codes later.)

Choose which codes are appropriate for you.

- ✓: If correct put a check mark above correct sound/word **(score 1)**
- **abc:** If incorrect put a line through the sound/word and write above what was said. **(no score)**
- **DK:** I don't know/no response **("record" and no score)**
- **SC:** Reader self-corrected **("record" and give 1 point)**
- **SO:** Sounded out and read correctly **("record" and give 1 point)**
- **MW:** Missed out a word **("record" and no score)**
- **UH:** Added sound /uh/ after consonant sound **("record" and give 1 point)**
- **AD:** Added a sound: "pond" for "pod" **(no score)**
- **OM:** Omitted a sound: "wet" for "went" **(no score)**
- **VE:** Visual error: "bat" for "pat" **(no score)**
- **GU:** Guessed the word **(no score)**
- **BL:** Sounds out but blends incorrectly **(no score)**

Name: **Date:**

1. Single sounds

Stage 1	S m t M i A T a s I
Stage 2	P n O p N o
Stage 3	g B h H c G b C
Stage 4	f V d E v F D e
Stage 5	K r L u k R l U
Stage 6	j Z w J z W
Stage 7	ff y ss ll x zz

Comments:

1. Single sounds

DK:

SC:

VE:

UH:

1. Single sounds

1st attempt /52

2nd attempt /52

3rd attempt /52

Name: **Date:**

2. Single words

Stage 1	sat	Sam	sit	mat
Stage 2	not	pat	nip	pot
Stage 3	hob	big	hat	cat
Stage 4	van	fig	man	bed
Stage 5	kid	run	let	bug
Stage 6	win	jug	zap	jet
Stage 7	off	yell	buzz	tax
	lass	mix	yes	will

Comments:

2. Single words

DK: OM:

SC: VE:

SO: BL:

AD:

2. Single words

1st attempt /32

2nd attempt /32

3rd attempt /32

Name: **Date:**

High-frequency words:

and the to a said into of

(We are not testing high-frequency words. They are here for you to note whether or not they are recognized by the reader.)

3. Text

Kim and Jess sat in the hot sun.

"Let us run to the hut to get a hat!" said Jess.

Kim had a cap in a bag and Jess had a hat in a box.

Jess got the hat but it fell on the mat.

Cal, the pup, ran into the hut and got the hat.

The pup ran off in a zig zag and hid in the van.

Yes, the pup had a lot of fun.

Will Jess get mad at Cal?

Comments:	3. Text		3. Text	
	DK:	OM:	1st attempt	/83
	SC:	VE:	2nd attempt	/83
	SO:	GU:	3rd attempt	/83
	MW:	BL:		
	AD:			

Name: **Date:**

4. Comprehension questions

1. Why did Kim and Jess need a hat?
2. Where did the hat fall?
3. Who ran off with the hat?
4. Why did Cal hide in a van?

Scores	1st attempt	2nd attempt	3rd attempt
1. Single sounds			
2. Single words			
3. Text			
4. Comprehension			
Total Score / 167			

% score reading text:

% score whole test:

Letter sounds

S	m	t	M	i	A
T	a	s	I	P	n
O	p	N	o	g	B
h	H	c	G	b	C
f	V	d	E	v	F
D	e	K	r	L	u
k	R	l	U	j	Z
w	J	z	W	ff	y

ss	ll	x	zz

Single words

sat	Sam	sit	mat
not	pat	nip	pot
hob	big	hat	cat
van	fig	man	bed
kid	run	let	bug
win	jug	zap	jet
off	yell	buzz	tax
lass	mix	yes	will

High-frequency words

and	the	to	a	said	into	of

Text

Kim and Jess sat in the hot sun.

"Let us run to the hut to get a hat!" said Jess.

Kim had a cap in a bag and Jess had a hat in a box.

Jess got the hat but it fell on the mat.

Cal, the pup, ran into the hut and got the hat.

The pup ran off in a zig zag and hid in the van.

Yes, the pup had a lot of fun.

Will Jess get mad at Cal?

Reading Assessment

Dandelion Series

ASSESSMENT FOR DANDELION LAUNCHERS: STAGES 8–10

1. CVCC, CCVC, CCVCC, CVCCC, and CCCVC words
2. Text with the spellings listed above

Response to reading: (For "record" write the appropriate code whilst testing; add the other codes later.)

Choose which codes are appropriate for you.

- ✓: If correct put a check mark above correct sound/word **(score 1)**
- ~~abc~~**:** If incorrect put a line through the sound/word and write above what was said. **(no score)**
- **DK:** I don't know/no response **("record" and no score)**
- **SC:** Reader self-corrected **("record" and give 1 point)**
- **SO:** Sounded out and read correctly **("record" and give 1 point)**
- **MW:** Missed out a word **("record" and no score)**
- **UH:** Added sound /uh/ after consonant sound **("record" and give 1 point)**
- **AD:** Added a sound: "pond" for "pod" **(no score)**
- **OM:** Omitted a sound: "wet" for "went" **(no score)**
- **VE:** Visual error: "bat" for "pat" **(no score)**
- **GU:** Guessed the word **(no score)**
- **BL:** Sounds out but blends incorrectly **(no score)**

Name: **Date:**

1. Stage 8: Single VCC and CVCC words

dust	zinc	ink	belt
just	desk	bulb	and
hump	vest	soft	wept
yelp	hulk	band	cups

Comments:	1. Single VCC and CVCC words	1. Single VCC and CVCC words
	DK:	1st attempt /16
	SC:	2nd attempt /16
	SO:	3rd attempt /16
	AD:	
	OM:	
	VE:	
	BL:	

Name: **Date:**

1. Stage 9: Single CCVC words

blot	twig	slug	grim
cliff	swum	spot	flag
smell	plot	skid	dwell
frog	glad	dress	snug

Comments:	1. Single CCVC words DK: SC: SO: AD: OM: VE: BL:	1. Single CCVC words 1st attempt /16 2nd attempt /16 3rd attempt /16

Name: **Date:**

1. Stage 10: Single CCVCC words

bland	stomp	glint	skunk
swift	spend	clamp	stops
scamp	frost	crept	plump
drink	trend	grunt	swept
claps	slept	skimp	crust

Comments:	1. Single CCVCC words	1. Single CCVCC words
	DK:	1st attempt /20
	SC:	2nd attempt /20
	SO:	3rd attempt /20
	AD:	
	OM:	
	VE:	
	BL:	

Name: **Date:**

1. Stage 10: Single CVCCC words

hands	limps	jumps	melts
ramps	sinks	costs	tilts

Comments:	1. Single CVCCC words		1. Single CVCCC words	
	DK:	OM:	1st attempt	/8
	SC:	VE:	2nd attempt	/8
	SO:	BL:	3rd attempt	/8
	AD:			

1. Stage 10: Single CCCVC words

scram	strip	scrub	scrap

Comments:	1. Single CCCVC words		1. Single CCCVC words	
	DK:	OM:	1st attempt	/4
	SC:	VE:	2nd attempt	/4
	SO:	BL:	3rd attempt	/4
	AD:			

Name: **Date:**

High-frequency words:

for to the out of

(We are not testing high-frequency words. They are here for you to note whether or not they are recognized by the reader.)

2. Text

Dad set up a tent for Gwen next to the hut.

The tent had a camp bed. Gwen sat on it.

Jed, the pet dog, crept up to the tent and went in to jump on Gwen.

Gwen held a hand up to stop him and fell off the camp bed.

In a blink, a brisk wind swept the camp bed on top of Gwen and Jed.

Jed slunk off out of the tent.

Gwent had a cut on her leg and went to get help from Dad.

Comments:	2. Text		2. Text	
	DK:	VE:	1st attempt	/88
	SC:	BL:	2nd attempt	/88
	SO:		3rd attempt	/88
	AD:			
	OM:			

Name: **Date:**

3. Comprehension questions

1. Where did Dad set up the tent?
2. Why did Gwen put her hand up?
3. Why did Gwen ask Dad for help?
4. How do you think Gwen felt about her camping experience?

Comments:	3. Comprehension		3. Comprehension	
	DK:	OM:	1st attempt	/4
	SC:	VE:	2nd attempt	/4
	SO:	BL:	3rd attempt	/4
	AD:			

Scores	1st attempt	2nd attempt	3rd attempt
1. Single words			
2. Text			
3. Comprehension			
Total Score / 156			

% score reading text:

% score whole test:

Single VCC and CVCC words

dust	zinc	ink	belt
just	desk	bulb	and
hump	vest	soft	wept
yelp	hulk	band	cups

Single CCVC words

blot	twig	slug	grim
cliff	swum	spot	flag
smell	plot	skid	dwell
frog	glad	dress	snug

Single CCVCC words

bland	stomp	glint	skunk
swift	spend	clamp	stops
scamp	frost	crept	plump
drink	trend	grunt	swept
claps	slept	skimp	crust

Single CVCCC words

hands	limps	jumps	melts
ramps	sinks	costs	tilts

Single CCCVC words

scram	strip	scrub	scrap

High-frequency words

a	for	to	the	out	of

Text

Dad set up a tent for Gwen next to the hut.

The tent had a camp bed. Gwen sat on it.

Jed, the pet dog, crept up to the tent and went in to jump on Gwen. Gwen held a hand up to stop him and fell off the camp bed.

In a blink, a brisk wind swept the camp bed on top of Gwen and Jed.

Jed slunk off out of the tent.

Gwen had a cut on her leg and went to get help from Dad.

Reading Assessment

Dandelion Series

ASSESSMENT FOR DANDELION LAUNCHERS: STAGES 11–15

1. Words with consonant digraphs ch, sh, th, ck, wh, and ng and spellings qu and ve
2. Texts with the spellings listed above.

Response to reading: (For "record" write the appropriate code whilst testing; add the other codes later.)

Choose which codes are appropriate for you.

- ✓: If correct put a check mark above correct sound/word **(score 1)**
- ~~abc~~**:** If incorrect put a line through the sound/word and write above what was said. **(no score)**
- **DK:** I don't know/no response **("record" and no score)**
- **SC:** Reader self-corrected **("record" and give 1 point)**
- **SO:** Sounded out and read correctly **("record" and give 1 point)**
- **MW:** Missed out a word **("record" and no score)**
- **UH:** Added sound /uh/ after consonant sound **("record" and give 1 point)**
- **AD:** Added a sound: "pond" for "pod" **(no score)**
- **OM:** Omitted a sound: "wet" for "went" **(no score)**
- **VE:** Visual error: "bat" for "pat" **(no score)**
- **GU:** Guessed the word **(no score)**
- **BL:** Sounds out but blends incorrectly **(no score)**

Name: **Date:**

1. Single words

chat	mush	this	rock
bang	when	fish	much
quit	moth	ship	king
bunch	then	luck	quick
crash	truck	broth	swing
chimp	shrub	throb	chick

Comments:	1. Single words	1. Single words
	DK:	1st attempt /24
	SC:	2nd attempt /24
	SO:	3rd attempt /24
	AD:	
	OM:	
	VE:	
	BL:	

Name: **Date:**

High-frequency words:

said to is be a the his no

(We are not testing high-frequency words. They are here for you to note whether or not they are recognized by the reader.)

2. Text

Jill said to Mick, "Which is the bus?"

"Quick!" said Mick. "That bus! It will not be a long trip to get to the ranch!"

Jill and Mick had to rush to get on the bus. Mick flung his bag on the bench next to Jill.

When Mick got his lunch box from his bag, the bus had to stop fast. Mick's lunch box fell off his lap with a thud.

Both Jill and Mick had to pick up the mess and dash off the bus with no lunch.

Comments:	2. Text		2. Text	
	DK:	OM:	1st attempt	/88
	SC:	VE:	2nd attempt	/88
	SO:	GU:	3rd attempt	/88
	MW:	BL:		
	AD:			

Name: **Date:**

3. Comprehension questions

1. Where were Mick and Jill going?
2. What did Mick have in his bag?
3. Why did the lunch box fall on the floor?
4. How do you think Mick felt when the lunch box fell on the floor?

Comments:	3. Comprehension		3. Comprehension	
	DK:	OM:	1st attempt	/4
	SC:	VE:	2nd attempt	/4
	SO:	BL:	3rd attempt	/4
	AD:			

Scores	1st attempt	2nd attempt	3rd attempt
1. Single words			
2. Text			
3. Comprehension			
Total Score / 116			

% score reading text:

% score whole test:

Single words

chat	mush	this	rock
bang	when	fish	much
quit	moth	ship	king
bunch	then	luck	quick
crash	truck	broth	swing
chimp	shrub	throb	chick

High-frequency words

said to is be a the his no

Text

Jill said to Mick, "Which is the bus?"

"Quick!" said Mick. "That bus! It will not be a long trip to get to the ranch!"

Jill and Mick had to rush to get on the bus. Mick flung his bag on the bench next to Jill.

When Mick got his lunch box from his bag, the bus had to stop fast. Mick's lunch box fell off his lap with a thud.

Both Jill and Mick had to pick up the mess and dash off the bus with no lunch.

Reading Assessment

Dandelion Series

ASSESSMENT FOR DANDELION READERS: VCe SPELLINGS

1. VCe spellings a–e, e–e, i–e, o–e, and u–e
2. Texts with the spellings listed above

Response to reading: (For "record" write the appropriate code whilst testing; add the other codes later.)

Choose which codes are appropriate for you.

- ✓: If correct put a check mark above correct sound/word **(score 1)**
- ~~**abc**~~**:** If incorrect put a line through the sound/word and write above what was said. **(no score)**
- **DK:** I don't know/no response **("record" and no score)**
- **SC:** Reader self-corrected **("record" and give 1 point)**
- **SO:** Sounded out and read correctly **("record" and give 1 point)**
- **MW:** Missed out a word **("record" and no score)**
- **UH:** Added sound /uh/ after consonant sound **("record" and give 1 point)**
- **AD:** Added a sound: "pond" for "pod" **(no score)**
- **OM:** Omitted a sound: "wet" for "went" **(no score)**
- **VE:** Visual error: "bat" for "pat" **(no score)**
- **GU:** Guessed the word **(no score)**
- **BL:** Sounds out but blends incorrectly **(no score)**

Name: **Date:**

1. Single words: a–e, e–e, i–e, o–e, and u–e

make	snake	plate	tale
inflate	these	eve	theme
meme	delete	athlete	smile
tile	pipe	stripe	bone
stone	globe	joke	flute
cube	plume	rule	volume

Comments:	1. Single words	1. Single words
	DK:	1st attempt /24
	SC:	2nd attempt /24
	SO:	3rd attempt /24
	AD:	
	OM:	
	VE:	
	BL:	

Name: **Date:**

High-frequency words:

is be to I put was my

(We are not testing high-frequency words. They are here for you to note whether or not they are recognized by the reader.)

2. Text

It is June. Pete will be ten. Eve and Steve want to make him a cake.

"Let's compete," said Eve. "I bet I bake the best cake."

"Fine," said Steve. "But I will win!"

The list told them what to include. Steve broke three an egg and dropped it into the bowl. Eve broke six eggs! Steve put in a bit of cake mix. Eve put in a pile.

"I will use the most," she said. "Then my cake will be the biggest!"

The cakes began to bake. Eve's cake began to rise, and rise, and rise… it was going to explode!

"Oh no!" Eve said. "It is like slime!"

Steve was serene. "What is my prize?"

"You get to wipe up the mess," Eve joked.

Comments:	2. Text		2. Text	
	DK:	OM:	1st attempt	/127
	SC:	VE:	2nd attempt	/127
	SO:	BL:	3rd attempt	/127
	AD:			

Name: **Date:**

3. Comprehension questions

1. How old is Pete going to be?
2. Why did Eve want to make the biggest cake?
3. Why do you think the cake exploded?
4. What was Steve's prize?

Comments:	3. Comprehension		3. Comprehension	
	DK:	OM:	1st attempt	/4
	SC:	VE:	2nd attempt	/4
	SO:	BL:	3rd attempt	/4
	AD:			

Scores	1st attempt	2nd attempt	3rd attempt
1. Single words			
2. Text			
3. Comprehension			
Total Score / 155			

% score reading text:

% score whole test:

Single words

make	snake	plate	tale
inflate	these	gene	theme
meme	delete	athlete	smile
tile	pipe	stripe	bone
stone	globe	joke	flute
cube	plume	rule	volume

High-frequency words

is be to I put was my

Text

It is June. Pete will be ten. Eve and Steve want to make him a cake.

"Let's compete," said Eve. "I bet I bake the best cake."

"Fine," said Steve. "But I will win!"

The list told them what to include. Steve broke an egg and dropped it into the bowl. Eve broke six eggs! Steve put in a bit of cake mix. Eve put in a pile.

"I will use the most," she said. "Then my cake will be the biggest!"

The cakes began to bake. Eve's cake began to rise, and rise, and rise... it was going to explode!

"Oh no!" Eve said. "It is like slime!"

Steve was serene. "What is my prize?"

"You get to wipe up the mess," Eve joked.

LESSON PLANS

Stage 1: s, a, t, i, m

STEP 1
Preparation

15 mins

Learning goal (2 mins)

- Explain the lesson goal. For example: "Today, we are going to be learning the new sounds /s/ /a/ /t/ /i/ /m/ and starting to read and make words such as 'sit' and 'mat.'"
- Show the book Dandelion Launchers Book 1a: Sam, Tam, Tim.
- You will be completing some activities from Dandelion Launchers Stages 1–7 Activities.

Preparation (18 mins)

- Introduce the new focus sounds: /s/ /a/ /t/ /i/ /m/ using sounds cards (Activities, page 24).
- Show the students the sound card with the letter 's.' Model how to say the sound correctly ask students to copy.
- Have students watch you as they say /s/.
- Repeat this process with /a/ /t/ /i/ and /m/.

Word building and blending

- First demonstrate how to build a word. Use only three sound cards, e.g. for the word "sit."
- Draw three lines on the whiteboard, and tell the students that you are going to show them how to build the word "sit."
- As you say the word slowly, move your finger under the lines.
- Ask the students to listen to the first sound in the word "sit"—point to the first line. Emphasize the first sound as you say the whole word. The students respond—/s/.
- Then ask the students which letter spells the sound /s/. The students point to the letter (or you can tell them). Bring the letter down to the first line.
- Repeat with the second and last sounds in the word. Now ask the students to sound all three sounds and blend them into a word, moving your finger under the word: /s/ /i/ /t/ → "sit."

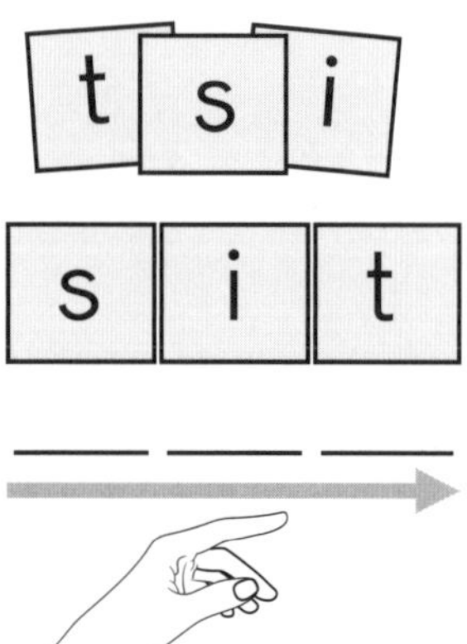

LESSON RESOURCES

Extension activities

1 Word reading

- Write the words you have created on the whiteboard. Then ask students to blend and read the words.
- Show how to say each sound individually and then blend them together to read the word. Model blending by using a swishing motion with your finger for blending.

2 Oral segmenting

- Say a word aloud (e.g. "sit") and ask students to a count the sounds in the word (3). Write the number of lines you need for all the sounds. Now ask students to listen to the sounds in the word and write a letter for every sound in the word as you spell the word.

3 Word chain

- Using sound cards or magnetic letters, demonstrate how to build the word "it." Explain to the students that you will be making one change to the word. They must be "sound detectives" and notice if you have added a sound, taken away a sound, or swapped a sound.
- Say that you are going to change the word "it" (moving your finger under the word) to "at." Ask the students to listen carefully to where the change has occurred. Move your finger under the words as you say it slowly. Once the change has been identified, invite a student to swap the letter card or letter. Ask all the students to sound out the word and read the new word, e.g. /a/ /t/ → "at."
- Introduce the new sounds gradually.
- Direct students through the following word-chain sequence: it—at—am—Sam—sat—sit—it

4 Reading game

- Play the game in Book 1a: Sam, Tam, Tim (pages 7–8) to familiarize students with the vocabulary in the book.

STEP 2
Application for reading

15 mins

Before reading (5 mins)

- Revisit the vocabulary taught in Step 1 (e.g. "mat"). Clearly say the word: /m/ /a/ /t/.
- Then provide a simple definition, for example, "A mat is fabric we put on the floor."
- Ask questions such as "What is a mat?" and "Where can we put a mat?"
- Then write the word on the whiteboard and refer back to it throughout the week for reinforcement.
- You could also draw a picture of a mat on the whiteboard or show an actual picture.

Application (10 mins)

- Once students have started to learn and blend words using the sounds learned in this lesson plan, it's important to provide them with opportunities for them to use their newly acquired skills.
- The chosen text for this reading activity is Book 1a: Sam, Tam, Tim. Briefly introduce the book, its characters, and its context to spark interest and set the stage for engagement.
- Lead students through a directed reading of Book 1a: Sam, Tam, Tim. Encourage students to sound out each word carefully and then blend the sounds together to form the word.
- Provide support by modeling the blending. This hands-on practice is crucial for reinforcing phonetic skills and building fluency.
- Encourage students to sound out each word and then blend to read. This is crucial for reinforcing their learning and for building their confidence.

Extension activities

- Following the initial reading, revisit Book 1a: Sam, Tam, Tim with a focus on fluency.
- Reading the book again allows students to practice their newly acquired skills, this time with an emphasis on reading more smoothly and confidently.
- Create an interactive reading environment by inviting students to take turns reading aloud. Encourage them to point to each word as they read.
- As students read more fluently, support them to read with more expression and prosody, changing their pitch, pace, and emphasis according to the words and punctuation.
- As well as enhancing reading fluency, directed practice introduces students to the expressive potential of reading aloud.

STEP 3
Application for spelling

15 mins

Segmenting and spelling (5 mins)

- Ask students to complete the following: **Fill in the missing sounds** (Activities, page 9).
- Demonstrate correct pencil grip to the class. The pencil should rest comfortably between the thumb and index finger, supported by the middle finger, with the other two fingers curled inwards. The student should have their hands resting on the table and their feet planted squarely on the floor; the paper should be at a slight angle. The student should learn to move the pencil forward using their hand muscles.
- Distribute the **Fill in the missing sounds** activity to each student.
- Instruct students to look at each picture and use it to determine the missing sound in the corresponding word.
- Encourage the students to say the sounds as they write them and then blend the three sounds in each word together as they write them.
- After students complete the activity, individually model the formation of each letter that was filled in during the activity on the whiteboard. Focus on the starting point, stroke direction, and completion of each letter.

Sentence dictation (10 mins)

- Read out the **Sentence dictation** sentences (Activities, page 35): "I am Sam." and "Sam sat." Encourage the students to sound out the words as they spell them.

Extension activities

- Ask students to complete **Fill in all the missing sounds** (Activities, page 10).
- Ask students to complete the **Matching lower to upper game** (Activities, page 12) to match lower to upper case letters.
- Remind students how to segment the sounds in each word to spell them.
- For students who finish early or need additional practice with letter formation, provide extra activity sheets with different words or have them create their own "missing sound" examples using words from a word bank.
- Additionally, you can create your own sentences using the learned sounds and dictate them for the students to spell.

STEP 4
Comprehension and consolidation
15 mins

Book reading (5 mins)

- Reread Book 1a: Sam, Tam, Tim.
- Revisiting the book helps to reinforce familiarity with the text and supports phonetic recognition and comprehension.

Sequencing (5 mins)

- For this activity, the students are going to retell the story, using the pictures and words in the **Retelling the story** activity (Activities, page 16).
- Divide students into small groups.
- Decide whether to number the cards on the back to make sequencing easier for the students.
- Provide each group with a set of cards. Encourage collaboration as they work together to place the picture cards in the correct order of the story.
- Invite each group to retell the story using their arranged cards. Encourage them to use the word cards to narrate the story.
- Alternatively, after sequencing the story, the students can use the word cards to reinforce vocabulary. Ask students to match the word cards to the corresponding picture cards, promoting word recognition and comprehension.

Comprehension (5 mins)

- Check students have understood the story by completing the **Comprehension** activity (Activities, page 18).
- The aim of this activity is to reinforce vocabulary and story comprehension through a matching exercise.
- Distribute the activity sheet to each student or small group.
- Cut out the words on the page. Then ask students to read and match them to the correct pictures.
- After matching, facilitate a discussion where students share their matches and explain their reasoning.

Extension activities

- Divide the class into pairs and give each pair a copy of the **Dice game** (Activities, page 22).
- Have students find and point to these words in Book 1a: Sam, Tam, Tim: "Sam," "Tim," "Tam," "mat," and "sit."

STEP 5
Tracking progress

- Complete the **Bookmark** (Activities, page 21) to make a quick, formative assessment of students' progress.
- Hide the words and ask students to write them out as you read them, encouraging them to segment each sound.
- Depending on your findings, either revisit some of the activities to reinforce any specific skill gaps, or invite students to complete an extension activity.

Extension activities

- Play the **Stepping stones game** (Activities, page 20).
- This game is suitable for 1–4 players and requires counters and a die.
- Students place their counters at the start of the stepping stones path. They then take turns rolling the die. They move their counter according to the number rolled.
- Upon landing on a stepping stone, the student reads the word or letter sound on that stone aloud.
- If a student lands on a stone with a directional arrow, they follow the arrow forward or backward.
- The first student to reach the end of the stepping stones path wins.
- Provide positive feedback and encouragement throughout the game.
- For those needing more support, help them to blend the letter sound or word with assistance.

PARALLEL BOOKS

In addition to Book 1a: Sam, Tam, Tim, the following books also cover the focus sounds (/s/ /a/ /t/ /i/ /m/) and can be used for more practice of decoding, for book bags to take home.

Dandelion Launchers

Book 1b: Pip and the Bat

Book 1b: Is it Sam?

Dandelion Launchers Extras

Book 1a: I am Sam

Book 1b: On the Mat

Dandelion World

Book 1a: Sit, Tim

Book 1b: At a Mat

Dandelion Readers

Book 1: Sam (Set 1 Units 1–10)

Book 1: Sam and Tim (Set 2 Units 1–10)

Book 3: A Hot Cab (Set 3 Units 1–10)

LESSON PLANS

Stage 2: n, o, p

STEP 1
Preparation

20 mins

Reviewing sounds (3 mins)

- Using sound cards, review some of the previously learned sounds: /s/ /a/ /t/ /i/ /m/. For example, model blending "mat," reading it sound by sound and then the whole word. /m/ /a/ /t/ → "mat."

Learning goal (2 mins)

- Explain to the students that you will be teaching them to read and spell new words using the new sounds /n/ /o/ /p/ and the sounds they have previously learned.
- Introduce the book Dandelion Launchers Book 2a: Pam.
- You will be completing some activities from Dandelion Launchers Stages 1–7 Activities.

Preparation (15 mins)

- Model the new focus sounds: /n/ /o/ /p/

Word building and blending

- First demonstrate how to build a word. Use only three sound cards, e.g. for "map."
- Draw three lines on the whiteboard, and tell the students that you are going to show them how to build the word "map."
- As you say the word slowly, move your finger under the lines.
- Ask the students to listen to the first sound in the word "map"—point to the first line. Emphasize the first sound as you say the whole word. The students respond—/m/.
- Then ask the students which letter spells the sound /m/. The students point to the letter (or you can tell them). Bring the letter down to the first line.
- Repeat with the second and last sounds in the word. Now ask the students to sound all three sounds and blend them into a word, moving your finger under the word: /m/ /a/ /p/ → "map."

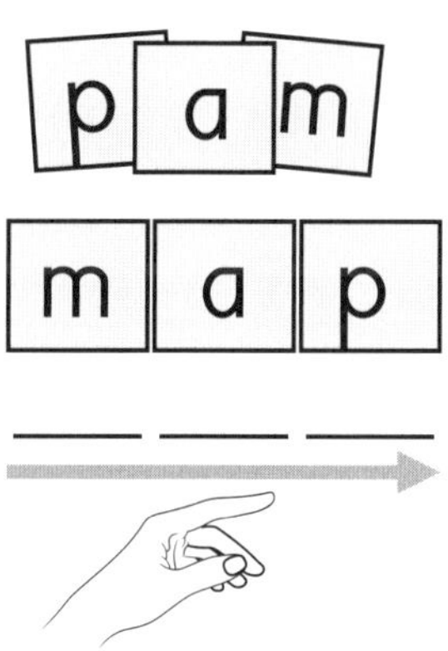

LESSON RESOURCES

Extension activities

1 Word reading

- Write the words you have created on the whiteboard. Then ask students to blend and read the words.
- Show how to say each sound individually and then blend them together to read the word. Model blending by pointing using a swishing motion with your finger.

2 Oral segmenting

- Say a word aloud (e.g. "pot") and ask pupils to count the sounds in the word (3). Write the number of lines you need for all the sounds. Now ask pupils to listen to the sounds in the word and write a letter for every sound in the word as you spell the word.

3 Word chain

- Using sound cards or magnetic letters, demonstrate how to build the word "pip." Explain to the students that you will be making one change to the word. They must be "sound detectives" and notice if you have added a sound, taken away a sound, or swapped a sound.
- Say that you are going to change the word "pip" (moving your finger under the word) to "pit." Ask the students to listen carefully to where the change has occurred. Move your finger under the words as you say it slowly. Once the change has been identified, invite a student to swap the sound card or letter. Ask all the students to sound out the word and read the new word, e.g. /p/ /i/ /t/ → "pit."
- Introduce the new sounds gradually. This allows students to incorporate the letters and sounds they have learned so far.
- Direct students through the following word-chain sequence: pip—pit—pin—pan—tan—tap—tip—pip

4 Reading game

- Play the game in Book 2a: Pam (pages 7–8) to familiarize students with the vocabulary in the book.

STEP 2
Application for reading
15 mins

Before reading (3 mins)

- Revisit the vocabulary taught in Step 1 (e.g. "pot"). Clearly say the word: /p/ /o/ /t/.
- Then provide a simple definition, for example, "A pot is a deep pan used for cooking."
- Ask questions such as "What can we put in a pot?"
- Then write the word on the whiteboard and refer back to it throughout the week for reinforcement.
- You could also draw a picture of a pot on the whiteboard or show an actual picture.

High-frequency words (2 mins)

- Pre-teach these high-frequency words: "a," "the," "is," and "and."
- Explain that these are high-frequency words that have tricky spellings the students will learn later. Read each high-frequency word aloud. Write the words on the board, showing the separate graphemes in each word.

Application (10 mins)

- The chosen text for this reading activity is Book 2a: Pam. Briefly introduce the book, its characters, and its context to spark interest and set the stage for engagement.
- Lead students through a directed reading of Book 2a: Pam. Encourage students to sound out each word carefully and then blend the sounds together to form the word.
- Provide support by modeling the blending. This hands-on practice is crucial for reinforcing phonetic skills and building fluency.
- Encourage students to sound out each word and then blend to read. This is crucial for reinforcing their learning and for building their confidence.

Extension activities

- Following the initial reading, revisit Book 2a: Pam with a focus on fluency.
- Reading the book again allows students to practice their newly acquired skills, this time with an emphasis on reading more smoothly and confidently.
- Create an interactive reading environment by inviting students to take turns reading aloud. Encourage them to point to each word as they read.
- As students read more fluently, support them to read with more expression and prosody, changing their pitch, pace, and emphasis according to the words and punctuation.

STEP 3
Application for spelling
15 mins

Segmenting and spelling (5 mins)

- Ask students to complete the following: **Fill in the missing sounds** (Activities, page 29).
- Demonstrate correct pencil grip to the class. The pencil should rest comfortably between the thumb and index finger, supported by the middle finger, with the other two fingers curled inwards. The student should have their hands resting on the table and their feet planted squarely on the floor; the paper should be at a slight angle. The student should learn to move the pencil forward using their hand muscles.
- Distribute the **Fill in the missing sounds** activity to each student.
- Instruct students to look at each picture and use it to determine the missing sound in the corresponding word.
- Encourage the students to say the sounds as they write them and then blend the three sounds in each word together as they write them.
- After students complete the activity, individually model the formation of each letter that was filled in during the activity on the whiteboard. Focus on the starting point, stroke direction, and completion of each letter.

Sentence dictation (10 mins)

- Read out the **Sentence dictation** sentences (Activities, page 35): "Pam is on top." and "A nap on the mat."
- Encourage the students to sound out the words as they spell them.

Extension activities

- Ask students to complete **Fill in all the missing sounds** (Activities, page 30) to practice writing whole words.
- Ask students to complete the **Fishing game** (Activities, page 34) to match lower to upper case letters.
- Remind students how to segment the sounds in each word to spell them.
- For students who finish early or need additional practice with letter formation, provide extra activity sheets with different words or have them create their own "missing sound" examples using words from a word bank.
- Additionally, you can create your own sentences using the learned sounds and dictate them for the students to spell.

STEP 4
Comprehension and consolidation

15 mins

Book reading (5 mins)

- Reread Book 2a: Pam.
- Revisiting the book helps to reinforce familiarity with the text and supports phonetic recognition and comprehension.

Sequencing (5 mins)

- For this activity, the students are going to retell the story, using the pictures and words in the **Retelling the story** activity (Activities, page 37).
- Divide students into small groups.
- Distribute the activity to each group.
- Decide whether to number the cards on the back to make sequencing easier for the students.
- Provide each group with a set of cards. Encourage collaboration as they work together to place the picture cards in the correct order of the story.
- Invite each group to retell the story using their arranged cards. Encourage them to use the word cards to narrate the story.
- Alternatively, after sequencing the story, the students can use the word cards to reinforce vocabulary. Ask students to match the word cards to the corresponding picture cards, promoting word recognition and comprehension.

Comprehension (5 mins)

- Check students have understood the story by completing the **Comprehension** activity (Activities, page 39).
- The aim of this activity is to reinforce vocabulary and story comprehension through a matching exercise.
- Distribute the activity to each student or small group.
- Cut out the words on the page. Then ask students to read and match them to the correct pictures.
- After matching, facilitate a discussion where students share their matches and explain their reasoning.

Extension activities

- Divide the class into pairs and give each pair a copy of the **Dice game** (Activities, page 43).
- Have students find and point to these words in Book 2a: Pam: "sit," "Pip," "top," and "pot."

STEP 5
Tracking progress

- Complete the **Bookmark** (Activities, page 42) to make a quick, formative assessment of students' progress.
- Hide the words and ask students to write them out as you read them, encouraging them to segment each sound.
- Depending on your findings, either revisit some of the activities to reinforce any specific skill gaps, or invite students to complete an extension activity.

Extension activities

- Play the **Stepping stones game** (Activities, page 41).
- This game is suitable for 1–4 players and requires counters and a die.
- Students place their counters at the start of the stepping stones path. They then take turns rolling the die. They move their counter according to the number rolled.
- Upon landing on a stepping stone, the student reads the word or letter sound on that stone aloud.
- If a student lands on a stone with a directional arrow, they follow the arrow forward or backward.
- The first student to reach the end of the stepping stones path wins.
- Provide positive feedback and encouragement throughout the game.
- For those needing more support, help them to blend the letter sound or word with assistance.

PARALLEL BOOKS

In addition to Book 2a: Pam, the following books also cover the focus sounds (/n/ /o/ /p/) and can be used for more practice of decoding, for book bags to take home.

Dandelion Launchers

Book 2b: The Pot

Dandelion Launchers Extras

Book 2a: A Man

Book 2b: A Map

Dandelion World

Book 2a: At the Top?

Book 2b: A Sap Tap

Dandelion Readers

Book 2: Pip (Set 1 Units 1–10)

Book 2: The Nap (Set 2 Units 1–10)

Book 2: Pip, Sam, and Tam (Set 3 Units 1–10)

LESSON PLANS

Stage 3: b, c, g, h

STEP 1 Preparation

20 mins

Reviewing sounds (3 mins)

- Using sound cards, review some of the previously learned sounds: /s/ /a/ /t/ /i/ /m/ /n/ /o/ /p/. For example, write the word "sip" on the whiteboard. Model blending "sip," reading it sound by sound and then the whole word. /s/ /i/ /p/ → "sip."

Learning goal (2 mins)

- Explain to the students that you will be teaching them to read and spell new words using the new sounds /b/ /c/ /g/ /h/ and the sounds they have previously learned.
- Introduce the book Dandelion Launchers Book 3a: Sam's Bag.
- You will be completing some activities from Dandelion Launchers Stages 1–7 Activities.

Preparation (15 mins)

- Model the new focus sounds: /b/ /c/ /g/ /h/

Word building and blending

- First demonstrate how to build a word. Use only three sound cards, e.g. for the word "hat."
- Draw three lines on the whiteboard, and tell the students that you are going to show them how to build the word "hat."
- As you say the word slowly, move your finger under the lines.
- Ask the students to listen to the first sound in the word "hat"—point to the first line. Emphasize the first sound as you say the whole word. The students respond—/h/.
- Then ask the students which letter spells the sound /h/. The students point to the letter (or you can tell them). Bring the letter down to the first line.
- Repeat with the second and last sounds in the word. Now ask the students to sound all three sounds and blend them into a word, moving your finger under the word: /h/ /a/ /t/ → "hat."

LESSON RESOURCES

Extension activities

1 Word reading

- Write the words you have created on the whiteboard. Then ask students to blend and read the words.
- Show how to say each sound individually and then blend them together to read the word. Model blending by using a swishing motion with your finger.

2 Oral segmenting

- Say a word aloud (e.g. "cog") and ask students to count the sounds in the word (3). Write the number of lines you need for all the sounds. Now ask students to listen to the sounds in the word and write a letter for every sound in the word as you spell the word.

3 Word chain

- Using sound cards or magnetic letters, demonstrate how to build the word "cat." Explain to the students that you will be making one change to the word. They must be "sound detectives" and notice if you have added a sound, taken away a sound, or swapped a sound.
- Say that you are going to change the word "cat" (moving your finger under the word) to "bat." Ask the students to listen carefully to where the change has occurred. Move your finger under the words as you say it slowly. Once the change has been identified, invite a student to swap the sound card or letter. Ask all the students to sound out the word and read the new word, e.g. /b/ /a/ /t/ → "bat."
- Introduce the new sounds gradually. This allows students to incorporate the letters and sounds they have learned so far.
- Direct students through the following word-chain sequence: cat—bat—hat—sat—pat—mat—tat—cat

4 Reading game

- Play the game in Book 3a: Sam's Bag (pages 7–8) to familiarize students with the vocabulary in the book.

STEP 2
Application for reading
15 mins

Before reading (3 mins)

- Revisit the vocabulary taught in Step 1 (e.g. "bag"). Clearly say the word: /b/ /a/ /g/
- Then provide a simple definition, for example, "A bag is used for carrying things."
- Ask questions such as, "What can we put in a bag?" Then write the word on the whiteboard and refer back to it throughout the week for reinforcement.
- You could also draw a picture of a bag on the whiteboard or show an actual picture.

High-frequency words (2 mins)

- Pre-teach and reiterate these high-frequency words: "Sam's," "has," "a," "get," "the," "is," and "Tam's."
- Explain that these are high-frequency words that have tricky spellings the students will learn later. Read each high-frequency word aloud. Write the words on the board, showing the separate graphemes in each word.

Application (10 mins)

- The chosen text for this reading activity is Book 3a: Sam's Bag. Briefly introduce the book, its characters, and its context to spark interest and set the stage for engagement.
- Lead students through a directed reading of Book 3a: Sam's Bag. Encourage students to sound out each word carefully and then blend the sounds together to form the word.
- Provide support by modeling the blending. This hands-on practice is crucial for reinforcing phonetic skills and building fluency.
- Encourage students to sound out each word and then blend to read. This is crucial for reinforcing their learning and for building their confidence.

Extension activities

- Following the initial reading, revisit Book 3a: Sam's Bag with a focus on fluency.
- Reading the book again allows students to practice their newly acquired skills, this time with an emphasis on reading more smoothly and confidently.
- Create an interactive reading environment by inviting students to take turns reading aloud. Encourage them to point to each word as they read.
- As students read more fluently, support them to read with more expression and prosody.

STEP 3
Application for spelling
15 mins

Segmenting and spelling (5 mins)

- Ask students to complete the following: **Fill in the missing sounds** (Activities, page 51).
- Demonstrate correct pencil grip to the class. The pencil should rest comfortably between the thumb and index finger, supported by the middle finger, with the other two fingers curled inwards. The student should have their hands resting on the table and their feet planted squarely on the floor; the paper should be at a slight angle. The student should learn to move the pencil forward using their hand muscles.
- Distribute the **Fill in the missing sounds** activity to each student.
- Instruct students to look at each picture and use it to determine the missing sound in the corresponding word.
- Encourage the students to say the sounds as they write them and then blend the three sounds in each word together as they write them.
- After students complete the activity, individually model the formation of each letter that was filled in during the activity on the whiteboard. Focus on the starting point, stroke direction, and completion of each letter.

Sentence dictation (10 mins)

- Read out the **Sentence dictation** sentences (Activities, page 57): "Sam, get the bag!" and "It is Tam's bag."
- Encourage the students to sound out the words as they spell them.

Extension activities

- Ask students to complete **Fill in all the missing sounds** (Activities, page 52) to practice writing whole words.
- Ask students to complete the **Matching lower to upper game** (Activities, page 55) to match lower to upper case letters.
- Remind students how to segment the sounds in each word to spell them.
- For students who finish early or need additional practice with letter formation, provide extra activity sheets with different words or have them create their own "missing sound" examples using words from a word bank.
- Additionally, you can create your own sentences using the learned sounds and dictate them for the students to spell.

STEP 4
Comprehension and consolidation

15 mins

Book reading (5 mins)

- Reread Book 3a: Sam's Bag.
- Revisiting the book helps to reinforce familiarity with the text and supports phonetic recognition and comprehension.

Sequencing (5 mins)

- For this activity, the students are going to retell the story, using the pictures and words in the **Retelling the story** activity (Activities, page 59).
- Divide students into small groups.
- Distribute the activity to each group.
- Decide whether to number the cards on the back to make sequencing easier for the students.
- Provide each group with a set of cards. Encourage collaboration as they work together to place the picture cards in the correct order of the story.
- Invite each group to retell the story using their arranged cards. Encourage them to use the word cards to narrate the story.
- Alternatively, after sequencing the story, the students can use the word cards to reinforce vocabulary. Ask students to match the word cards to the corresponding picture cards, promoting word recognition and comprehension.

Comprehension (5 mins)

- Check students have understood the story by completing the **Comprehension** activity (Activities, page 61).
- The aim of this activity is to reinforce vocabulary and story comprehension through a matching exercise.
- Distribute the activity to each student or small group.
- Cut out the words on the page. Then ask students to read and match them to the correct pictures.
- After matching, facilitate a discussion where students share their matches and explain their reasoning.

Extension activities

- Divide the class into pairs and give each pair a copy of the **Dice game** (Activities, page 67).
- Have students find and point to these words in Book 3a: Sam's Bag: "bag" and "big."

STEP 5
Tracking progress

- Complete the **Bookmark** (Activities, page 66) to make a quick, formative assessment of students' progress.
- Hide the words and ask students to write them out as you read them, encouraging them to segment each sound.
- Depending on your findings, either revisit some of the activities to reinforce any specific skill gaps, or invite students to complete an extension activity.

Extension activities

- Play the **Stepping stones game** (Activities, page 63).
- This game is suitable for 1–4 players and requires counters and a die.
- Students place their counters at the start of the stepping stones path. They then take turns rolling the die. They move their counter according to the number rolled.
- Upon landing on a stepping stone, the student reads the word or letter sound on that stone aloud.
- If a student lands on a stone with a directional arrow, they follow the arrow forward or backward.
- The first student to reach the end of the stepping stones path wins.
- Provide positive feedback and encouragement throughout the game.
- For those needing more support, help them to blend the letter sound or word with assistance.

PARALLEL BOOKS

In addition to Book 3a: Sam's Bag, the following books also cover the focus sounds (/b/ /c/ /g/ /h/) and can be used for more practice of decoding, for book bags to take home.

Dandelion Launchers

Book 3b: Pip and the Bat

Dandelion Launchers Extras

Book 3a: Bob

Book 3b: Pam and the Cat

Dandelion World

Book 3a: The Cat Can Tag

Book 3b: A Big Hat

Dandelion Readers

Book 3: In the Bag (Set 1 Units 1–10)

Book 3: In the Can (Set 2 Units 1–10)

Book 3: A Hot Cab (Set 3 Units 1–10)

LESSON PLANS

Stage 4: d, e, f, v

STEP 1
Preparation

20 mins

Reviewing sounds (3 mins)

- Using sound cards, review some of the previously learned sounds. For example, write the word "hip" on the whiteboard. Model blending "hip," reading it sound by sound and then the whole word. /h/ /i/ /p/ → "hip."

Learning goal (2 mins)

- Explain to the students that you will be teaching them to read and spell new words using the new sounds /d/ /e/ /f/ /v/ and the sounds they have previously learned.
- Introduce the book Dandelion Launchers Book 4a: Ted.
- You will be completing some activities from Dandelion Launchers Stages 1–7 Activities.

Preparation (15 mins)

- Model the new focus sounds: /d/ /e/ /f/ /v/

Word building and blending

- First demonstrate how to build a word. Use only three sound cards, e.g. for the word "dot."
- Draw three lines on the whiteboard, and tell the students that you are going to show them how to build the word "dot."
- As you say the word slowly, move your finger under the lines.
- Ask the students to listen to the first sound in the word "dot"—point to the first line. Emphasize the first sound as you say the whole word. The students respond—/d/.
- Then ask the students which letter spells the sound /d/. The students point to the letter (or you can tell them). Bring the letter down to the first line.
- Repeat with the second and last sounds in the word. Now ask the students to sound all three sounds and blend them into a word, moving your finger under the word: /d/ /o/ /t/ → "dot."

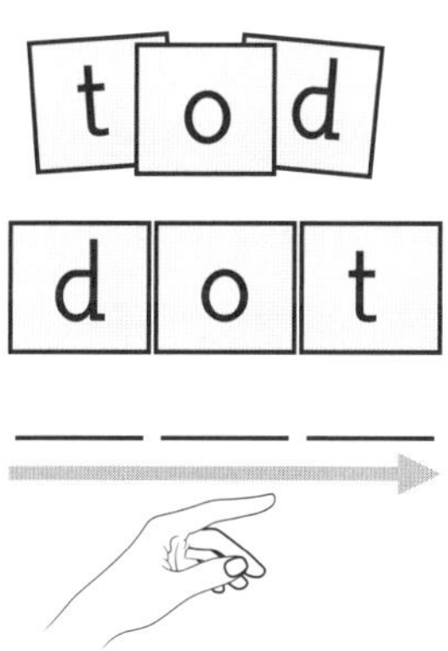

LESSON RESOURCES

Extension activities

1 Word reading

- Write the words you have created on the whiteboard. Then ask students to blend and read the words.
- Show how to say each sound individually and then blend them together to read the word. Model blending by using a swishing motion with your finger.

2 Oral segmenting

- Say a word aloud (e.g. "dot") and ask students to count the sounds in the word (3). Write the number of lines you need for all the sounds. Now ask students to listen to the sounds in the word and write a letter for every sound in the word as you spell the word.

3 Word chain

- Using sound cards or magnetic letters, demonstrate how to build the word "fed." Explain to the students that you will be making one change to the word. They must be "sound detectives" and notice if you have added a sound, taken away a sound, or swapped a sound.
- Say that you are going to change the word "fed" (moving your finger under the word) to "fad." Ask the students to listen carefully to where the change has occurred. Move your finger under the words as you say it slowly. Once the change has been identified, invite a student to swap the sound card or letter. Ask all the students to sound out the word and read the new word, e.g. /f/ /a/ /d/ → "fad."
- Introduce the new sounds gradually..
- Direct students through the following word-chain sequence: fed—fad—bad—sad—sat—set—get—vet—bet—bed—fed

4 Reading game

- Play the game in Book 4a: Ted (pages 7–8) to familiarize students with the vocabulary in the book.

STEP 2
Application for reading
15 mins

Before reading (3 mins)

- Revisit the vocabulary taught in Step 1 (e.g. "bed"). Clearly say the word: /b/ /e/ /d/
- Then provide a simple definition, for example, "A bed is a comfy place where we sleep."
- Ask questions such as "When do we use a bed?" and "What rhymes with 'bed'?"
- Then write the word on the whiteboard and refer back to it throughout the week for reinforcement.
- You could also draw a picture of a pot on the whiteboard or show an actual picture.

High-frequency words (2 mins)

- Pre-teach and reiterate these high-frequency words: "the," "up," "off," "into," "is," and "a."
- Explain that these are high-frequency words that have tricky spellings the students will learn later. Read each high-frequency word aloud. Write the words on the board, showing the separate graphemes in each word.

Application (10 mins)

- The chosen text for this reading activity is Book 4a: Ted. Briefly introduce the book, its characters, and its context to spark interest and set the stage for engagement.
- Lead students through a directed reading of Book 4a: Ted. Encourage students to sound out each word carefully and then blend the sounds together to form the word.
- Provide support by modeling the blending. This hands-on practice is crucial for reinforcing phonetic skills and building fluency.
- Encourage students to sound out each word and then blend to read. This is crucial for reinforcing their learning and for building their confidence.

Extension activities

- Following the initial reading, revisit Book 4a: Ted with a focus on fluency.
- Reading the book again allows students to practice their newly acquired skills, this time with an emphasis on reading more smoothly and confidently.
- Create an interactive reading environment by inviting students to take turns reading aloud. Encourage them to point to each word as they read.
- As students read more fluently, support them to read with more expression and prosody.

STEP 3
Application for spelling
15 mins

Segmenting and spelling (5 mins)

- Ask students to complete the following: **Fill in the missing sounds** (Activities, page 75).
- Demonstrate correct pencil grip to the class. The pencil should rest comfortably between the thumb and index finger, supported by the middle finger, with the other two fingers curled inwards. The student should have their hands resting on the table and their feet planted squarely on the floor; the paper should be at a slight angle. The student should learn to move the pencil forward using their hand muscles.
- Distribute the **Fill in the missing sounds** activity to each student.
- Instruct students to look at each picture and use it to determine the missing sound in the corresponding word.
- Encourage the students to say the sounds as they write them and then blend the three sounds in each word together as they write them.
- After students complete the activity, individually model the formation of each letter that was filled in during the activity on the whiteboard. Focus on the starting point, stroke direction, and completion of each letter.

Sentence dictation (10 mins)

- Read out the **Sentence dictation** sentences (Activities, page 81): "Viv got into bed." and "Ted is in the pit!"
- Encourage the students to sound out the words as they spell them.

Extension activities

- Ask students to complete **Fill in all the missing sounds** (Activities, page 76) to practice writing whole words.
- Ask students to complete the **Fishing game** (Activities, page 80) to match lower to upper case letters.
- Remind students how to segment the sounds in each word to spell them.
- For students who finish early or need additional practice with letter formation, provide extra activity sheets with different words or have them create their own "missing sound" examples using words from a word bank.
- Additionally, you can create your own sentences using the learned sounds and dictate them for the students to spell.

STEP 4
Comprehension and consolidation
15 mins

Book reading (5 mins)

- Reread Book 4a: Ted.
- Revisiting the book helps to reinforce familiarity with the text and supports phonetic recognition and comprehension.

Sequencing (5 mins)

- For this activity, the students are going to retell the story, using the pictures and words in the **Retelling the story** activity (Activities, page 83).
- Divide students into small groups.
- Distribute the activity to each group.
- Decide whether to number the cards on the back to make sequencing easier for the students.
- Provide each group with a set of cards. Encourage collaboration as they work together to place the picture cards in the correct order of the story.
- Invite each group to retell the story using their arranged cards. Encourage them to use the word cards to narrate the story.
- Alternatively, after sequencing the story, the students can use the word cards to reinforce vocabulary. Ask students to match the word cards to the corresponding picture cards, promoting word recognition and comprehension.

Comprehension (5 mins)

- Check students have understood the story by completing the **Comprehension** activity (Activities, page 85).
- The aim of this activity is to reinforce vocabulary and story comprehension through a matching exercise.
- Distribute the activity to each student or small group.
- Cut out the words on the page. Then ask students to read and match them to the correct pictures.
- After matching, facilitate a discussion where students share their matches and explain their reasoning.

Extension activities

- Divide the class into pairs and give each pair a copy of the **Dice game** (Activities, page 91).
- Have students find and point to these words in Book 4a: Ted: "set" and "bed."

STEP 5
Tracking progress

- Complete the **Bookmark** (Activities, page 90) to make a quick, formative assessment of students' progress.
- Hide the words and ask students to write them out as you read them, encouraging them to segment each sound.
- Depending on your findings, either revisit some of the activities to reinforce any specific skill gaps, or invite students to complete an extension activity.

Extension activities

- Play the **Stepping stones game** (Activities, page 89).
- This game is suitable for 1–4 players and requires counters and a die.
- Students place their counters at the start of the stepping stones path. They then take turns rolling the die. They move their counter according to the number rolled.
- Upon landing on a stepping stone, the student reads the word or letter sound on that stone aloud.
- If a student lands on a stone with a directional arrow, they follow the arrow forward or backward.
- The first student to reach the end of the stepping stones path wins.
- Provide positive feedback and encouragement throughout the game.
- For those needing more support, help them to blend the letter sound or word with assistance.

PARALLEL BOOKS

In addition to Book 4a: Ted, the following books also cover the focus sounds (/d/ /e/ /f/ /v/) and can be used for more practice of decoding, for book bags to take home.

Dandelion Launchers

Book 4b: Meg and Ted

Dandelion Launchers Extras

Book 4a: The Fib

Book 4b: Bob and the Cod

Dandelion World

Book 4a: Get Fed

Book 4b: A Vet in a Van

Dandelion Readers

Book 4: Bad Cat (Set 1 Units 1–10)

Book 4: At the Vet (Set 2 Units 1–10)

Book 4: In the Van (Set 3 Units 1–10)

Stage 5: k, l, r, u

STEP 1
Preparation

20 mins

Reviewing sounds (3 mins)

- Using sound cards, review some of the previously learned sounds. For example: model blending "fed," reading it sound by sound and then the whole word. /f/ /e/ /d/ → "fed."

Learning goals (2 mins)

- Explain to the students that you will be teaching them to read and spell new words using the new sounds /k/ /l/ /r/ /u/ and the sounds they have previously learned.
- Introduce the book Dandelion Launchers Book 5a: Ken, the Rat.
- You will be completing some activities from Dandelion Launchers Stages 1–7 Activities.

Preparation (15 mins)

- Model the new focus sounds: /k/ /l/ /r/ /u/

Word building and blending

- First demonstrate how to build a word. Use only three sound cards, e.g. for the word "rug."
- Draw three lines on the whiteboard, and tell the students that you are going to show them how to build the word "rug."
- As you say the word slowly, move your finger under the lines.
- Ask the students to listen to the first sound in the word "rug"—point to the first line. Emphasize the first sound as you say the whole word. The students respond—/r/.
- Then ask the students which letter spells the sound /r/. The students point to the letter (or you can tell them). Bring the letter down to the first line.
- Repeat with the second and last sounds in the word. Now ask the students to sound all three sounds and blend them into a word, moving your finger under the word: /r/ /u/ /g/ → "rug."

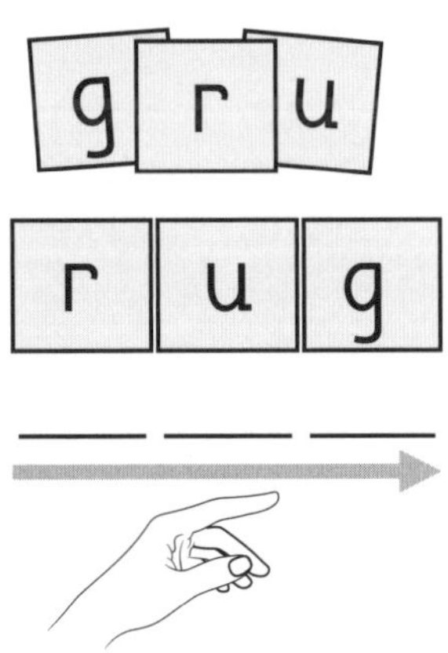

LESSON RESOURCES

Extension activities

1 Word reading

- Write the words you have created on the whiteboard. Then ask students to blend and read the words.
- Show how to say each sound individually and then blend them together to read the word. Model blending by using a swishing motion with your finger.

2 Oral segmenting

- Say a word aloud (e.g. "kit") and ask students to count the sounds in the word (3). Write the number of lines you need for all the sounds. Now ask students to listen to the sounds in the word and write a letter for every sound in the word as you spell the word.

3 Word chain

- Using sound cards or magnetic letters, demonstrate how to build the word "rag." Explain to the students that you will be making one change to the word. They must be "sound detectives" and notice if you have added a sound, taken away a sound, or swapped a sound.
- Say that you are going to change the word "rag" (moving your finger under the word) to "rug." Ask the students to listen carefully to where the change has occurred. Move your finger under the word as you say it slowly. Once the change has sound identified, invite a student to swap the sound card or letter. Ask all the students to sound out the word and read the new word, e.g. /r/ /u/ /g/ → "rug."
- Introduce the new sounds gradually.
- Direct students through the following word-chain sequence: rag—rug—lug—leg—keg—peg—pug—mug—rug—rag

4 Reading game

- Play the game in Book 5a: Ken, the Rat (pages 7–8) to familiarize students with the vocabulary in the book.

STEP 2
Application for reading
15 mins

Before reading (3 mins)

- Revisit the vocabulary taught in Step 1 (e.g. "rat"). Clearly say the word: /r/ /a/ /t/
- Then provide a simple definition, for example, "A rat is a small animal with a tail."
- Ask questions such as, "What rhymes with 'rat'?"
- Then write the word on the whiteboard and refer back to it throughout the week for reinforcement.
- You could also draw a picture of a rat on the whiteboard or show an actual picture.

High-frequency words (2 mins)

- Pre-teach and reiterate these high-frequency words: "the," "a," and "it's."
- Explain that these are high-frequency words that have tricky spellings the students will learn later. Read each high-frequency word aloud. Write the words on the board, showing the separate graphemes in each word.

Application (10 mins)

- The chosen text for this reading activity is Book 5a: Ken, the Rat. Briefly introduce the book, its characters, and its context to spark interest and set the stage for engagement.
- Lead students through a directed reading of Book 5a: Ken, the Rat. Encourage students to sound out each word carefully and then blend the sounds together to form the word.
- Provide support by modeling the blending. This hands-on practice is crucial for reinforcing phonetic skills and building fluency.
- Encourage students to sound out each word and then blend to read. This is crucial for reinforcing their learning and for building their confidence.

Extension activities

- Following the initial reading, revisit Book 5a: Ken, the Rat with a focus on fluency.
- Reading the book again allows students to practice their newly acquired skills, this time with an emphasis on reading more smoothly and confidently.
- Create an interactive reading environment by inviting students to take turns reading aloud. Encourage them to point to each word as they read.
- As students read more fluently, support them to read with more expression and prosody.

STEP 3
Application for spelling
15 mins

Segmenting and spelling (5 mins)

- Ask students to complete the following: **Fill in the missing sounds** (Activities, page 99).
- Demonstrate correct pencil grip to the class. The pencil should rest comfortably between the thumb and index finger, supported by the middle finger, with the other two fingers curled inwards. The student should have their hands resting on the table and their feet planted squarely on the floor; the paper should be at a slight angle. The student should learn to move the pencil forward using their hand muscles.
- Distribute the **Fill in the missing sounds** activity to each student.
- Instruct students to look at each picture and use it to determine the missing sound in the corresponding word.
- Encourage the students to say the sounds as they write them and then blend the three sounds in each word together as they write them.
- After students complete the activity, individually model the formation of each letter that was filled in during the activity on the whiteboard. Focus on the starting point, stroke direction, and completion of each letter.

Sentence dictation (10 mins)

- Read out the **Sentence dictation** sentences (Activities, page 105): "Ken got a red tan." and "Ken hid in a log."
- Encourage the students to sound out the words as they spell them.

Extension activities

- Ask students to complete **Fill in all the missing sounds** (Activities, page 100) to practice writing whole words.
- Ask students to complete the **Matching lower to upper game** (Activities, page 80) to match lower to upper case letters.
- Remind students how to segment the sounds in each word to spell them.
- For students who finish early or need additional practice with letter formation, provide extra activity sheets with different words or have them create their own "missing sound" examples using words from a word bank.
- Additionally, you can create your own sentences using the learned sounds and dictate them for the students to spell.

STEP 4
Comprehension and consolidation

15 mins

Book reading (5 mins)

- Reread Book 5a: Ken, the Rat.
- Revisiting the book helps to reinforce familiarity with the text and supports phonetic recognition and comprehension.

Sequencing (5 mins)

- For this activity, the students are going to retell the story, using the pictures and words in the **Retelling the story** activity (Activities, page 107).
- Divide students into small groups.
- Distribute the activity to each group.
- Decide whether to number the cards on the back to make sequencing easier for the students.
- Provide each group with a set of cards. Encourage collaboration as they work together to place the picture cards in the correct order of the story.
- Invite each group to retell the story using their arranged cards. Encourage them to use the word cards to narrate the story.
- Alternatively, after sequencing the story, the students can use the word cards to reinforce vocabulary. Ask students to match the word cards to the corresponding picture cards, promoting word recognition and comprehension.

Comprehension (5 mins)

- Check students have understood the story by completing the **Comprehension** activity (Activities, page 109).
- The aim of this activity is to reinforce vocabulary and story comprehension through a matching exercise.
- Distribute the activity to each student or small group.
- Cut out the words on the page. Then ask students to read and match them to the correct pictures.
- After matching, facilitate a discussion where students share their matches and explain their reasoning.

Extension activities

- Divide the class into pairs and give each pair a copy of the **Dice game** (Activities, page 115).
- Have students find and point to these words in Book 5a: Ken, the Rat: "rat," "sat," and "sun."

STEP 5
Tracking progress

- Complete the **Bookmark** (Activities, page 114) to make a quick, formative assessment of students' progress.
- Hide the words and ask students to write them out as you read them, encouraging them to segment each sound.
- Depending on your findings, either revisit some of the activities to reinforce any specific skill gaps, or invite students to complete an extension activity.

Extension activities

- Play the **Stepping stones game** (Activities, page 113).
- This game is suitable for 1–4 players and requires counters and a die.
- Students place their counters at the start of the stepping stones path. They then take turns rolling the die. They move their counter according to the number rolled.
- Upon landing on a stepping stone, the student reads the word or letter sound on that stone aloud.
- If a student lands on a stone with a directional arrow, they follow the arrow forward or backward.
- The first student to reach the end of the stepping stones path wins.
- Provide positive feedback and encouragement throughout the game.
- For those needing more support, help them to blend the letter sound or word with assistance.

PARALLEL BOOKS

In addition to Book 5a: Ken, the Rat, the following books also cover the focus sounds (/k/ /l/ /r/ /u/) and can be used for more practice of decoding, for book bags to take home.

Dandelion Launchers
Book 5b: Kim, the Bug

Dandelion Launchers Extras
Book 5a: The Bus
Book 5b: Mud

Dandelion World
Book 5a: Up on the Log
Book 5b: A Fun Kid

Dandelion Readers
Book 5: Bun in a Sun (Set 1 Units 1–10)
Book 5: Red Gum (Set 2 Units 1–10)
Book 5: The Hut (Set 3 Units 1–10)

Stage 6: j, w, z

STEP 1
Preparation

20 mins

LESSON RESOURCES

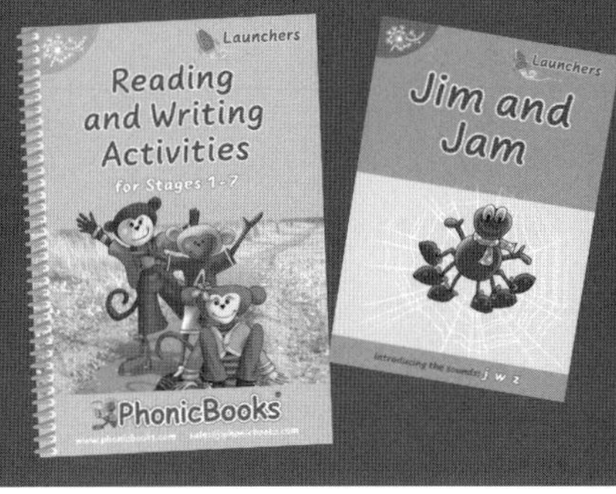

Reviewing sounds (3 mins)

- Using sound cards, review some of the previously learned sounds. For example: model blending "rug," reading it sound by sound and then the whole word. /r/ /u/ /g/ → "rug."

Learning goal (2 mins)

- Explain to the students that you will be teaching them to read and spell new words using the new sounds /j/ /w/ /z/ and the sounds they have previously learned.
- Introduce the book Dandelion Launchers Book 6a: Jim and Jam.
- You will be completing some activities from Dandelion Launchers Stages 1–7 Activities.

Preparation (15 mins)

- Model the new focus sounds: /j/ /w/ /z/

Word building and blending

- First demonstrate how to build a word. Use only three sound cards, e.g. for the word "wig."
- Draw three lines on the whiteboard, and tell the students that you are going to show them how to build the word "wig."
- As you say the word slowly, move your finger under the lines.
- Ask the students to listen to the first sound in the word "wig"—point to the first line. Emphasize the first sound as you say the whole word. The students respond—/w/.
- Then ask the students which letter spells the sound /w/. The students point to the letter (or you can tell them). Bring the letter down to the first line.
- Repeat with the second and last sounds in the word. Now ask the students to sound all three sounds and blend them into a word, moving your finger under the word: /w/ /i/ /g/ → "wig."

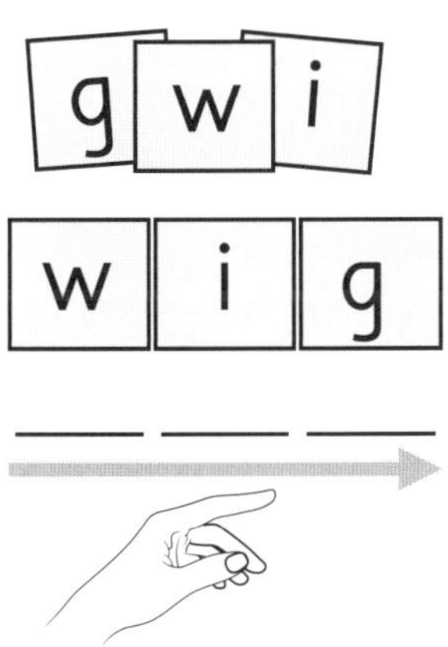

Extension activities

1 Word reading

- Write the words you have created on the whiteboard. Then ask students to blend and read the words.
- Show how to say each sound individually and then blend them together to read the word. Model blending by using a swishing motion with your finger.

2 Oral segmenting

- Say a word aloud (e.g. "zap") and ask students to count the sounds in the word (3). Write the number of lines you need for all the sounds. Now ask students to listen to the sounds in the word and write a letter for every sound in the word as you spell the word.

3 Word chain

- Using sound cards or magnetic letters, demonstrate how to build the word "zap." Explain to the students that you will be making one change to the word. They must be "sound detectives" and notice if you have added a sound, taken away a sound, or swapped a sound.
- Say that you are going to change the word "zap" (moving your finger under the word) to "zip." Ask the students to listen carefully to where the change has occurred. Move your finger under the words as you say it slowly. Once the change has been identified, invite a student to swap the sound card or letter. Ask all the students to sound out the word and read the new word, e.g. /z/ /a/ /p/ → "zip."
- Introduce the new sounds gradually.
- Direct students through the following word-chain sequence: zap—zip—pip—ip—wip—wep—wet—pet—pip—zip—zap

4 Reading game

- Play the game in Book 6a: Jim and Jam (pages 7–8) to familiarize students with the vocabulary in the book.

STEP 2
Application for reading
15 mins

Before reading (3 mins)

- Revisit the vocabulary taught in Step 1 (e.g. "web"). Clearly say the word: /w/ /e/ /b/
- Explore different meanings of the word "web". For example: "a spider's web" or "the internet."
- Then write the word on the whiteboard and refer back to it throughout the week for reinforcement.
- You could also draw a picture of a spider's web on the whiteboard or show an actual picture.

High-frequency words (2 mins)

- Pre-teach and reiterate these high-frequency words: "and," "was," "his," "I," "have", "a," "of," "to," "the," "legs," and "into."
- Explain that these are high-frequency words that have tricky spellings the students will learn later. Read each high-frequency word aloud. Write the words on the board, showing the separate graphemes in each word.

Application (10 mins)

- The chosen text for this reading activity is Book 6a: Jim and Jam. Briefly introduce the book, its characters, and its context to spark interest and set the stage for engagement.
- Lead students through a directed reading of Book 6a: Jim and Jam. Encourage students to sound out each word carefully and then blend the sounds together to form the word.
- Provide support by modeling the blending. This hands-on practice is crucial for reinforcing phonetic skills and building fluency.
- Encourage students to sound out each word and then blend to read. This is crucial for reinforcing their learning and for building their confidence.

Extension activities

- Following the initial reading, revisit Book 6a: Jim and Jam with a focus on fluency.
- Reading the book again allows students to practice their newly acquired skills, this time with an emphasis on reading more smoothly and confidently.
- Create an interactive reading environment by inviting students to take turns reading aloud. Encourage them to point to each word as they read.
- As students read more fluently, support them to read with more expression and prosody.

STEP 3
Application for spelling
15 mins

Segmenting and spelling (5 mins)

- Ask students to complete the following: **Fill in the missing sounds** (Activities, page 123).
- Demonstrate correct pencil grip to the class. The pencil should rest comfortably between the thumb and index finger, supported by the middle finger, with the other two fingers curled inwards. The student should have their hands resting on the table and their feet planted squarely on the floor; the paper should be at a slight angle. The student should learn to move the pencil forward using their hand muscles.
- Photocopy and distribute the **Fill in the missing sounds** activity to each student.
- Instruct students to look at each picture and use it to determine the missing sound in the corresponding word.
- Encourage the students to say the sounds as they write them and then blend the three sounds in each word together as they write them.
- After students complete the activity, individually model the formation of each letter that was filled in during the activity on the whiteboard. Focus on the starting point, stroke direction, and completion of each letter.

Sentence dictation (10 mins)

- Read out the **Sentence dictation** sentences (Activities, page 129): "Jim was in his big web." and "Jim got into a tub."
- Encourage the students to sound out the words as they spell them.

Extension activities

- Ask students to complete **Fill in all the missing sounds** (Activities, page 124) to practice writing whole words.
- Ask students to complete the **Fishing game** (Activities, page 128) to match lower to upper case letters.
- Remind students how to segment the sounds in each word to spell them.
- For students who finish early or need additional practice with letter formation, provide extra activity sheets with different words or have them create their own "missing sound" examples using words from a word bank.
- Additionally, you can create your own sentences using the learned sounds and dictate them for the students to spell.

STEP 4
Comprehension and consolidation

15 mins

Book reading (5 mins)

- Reread Book 6a: Jim and Jam.
- Revisiting the book helps to reinforce familiarity with the text and supports phonetic recognition and comprehension.

Sequencing (5 mins)

- For this activity, the students are going to retell the story, using the pictures and words in the **Retelling the story** activity (Activities, page 131).
- Divide students into small groups.
- Distribute the activity to each group.
- Decide whether to number the cards on the back to make sequencing easier for the students.
- Provide each group with a set of cards. Encourage collaboration as they work together to place the picture cards in the correct order of the story.
- Invite each group to retell the story using their arranged cards. Encourage them to use the word cards to narrate the story.
- Alternatively, after sequencing the story, the students can use the word cards to reinforce vocabulary. Ask students to match the word cards to the corresponding picture cards, promoting word recognition and comprehension.

Comprehension (5 mins)

- Check students have understood the story by completing the **Comprehension** activity (Activities, page 133).
- The aim of this activity is to reinforce vocabulary and story comprehension through a matching exercise.
- Distribute the activity to each student or small group.
- Cut out the words on the page. Then ask students to read and match them to the correct pictures.
- After matching, facilitate a discussion where students share their matches and explain their reasoning.

Extension activities

- Divide the class into pairs and give each pair a copy of the **Dice game** (Activities, page 139).
- Have students find and point to these words in Book 6a: Jim and Jam: "web," "jet," and "jam."

STEP 5
Tracking progress

- Complete the **Bookmark** (Activities, page 138) to make a quick, formative assessment of students' progress.
- Hide the words and ask students to write them out as you read them, encouraging them to segment each sound.
- Depending on your findings, either revisit some of the activities to reinforce any specific skill gaps, or invite students to complete an extension activity.

Extension activities

- Play the **Stepping stones game** (Activities, page 137).
- This game is suitable for 1–4 players and requires counters and a die.
- Students place their counters at the start of the stepping stones path. They then take turns rolling the die. They move their counter according to the number rolled.
- Upon landing on a stepping stone, the student reads the word or letter sound on that stone aloud.
- If a student lands on a stone with a directional arrow, they follow the arrow forward or backward.
- The first student to reach the end of the stepping stones path wins.
- Provide positive feedback and encouragement throughout the game.
- For those needing more support, help them to blend the letter sound or word with assistance.

PARALLEL BOOKS

In addition to Book 6a: Jim and Jam, the following books also cover the focus sounds (/j/ /w/ /z/) and can be used for more practice of decoding, for book bags to take home.

Dandelion Launchers

Book 6b: Ken Gets Wet

Dandelion Launchers Extras

Book 6a: Viv Can Run

Book 6b: A Bad Job

Dandelion World

Book 6a: Bug in a Jam

Book 6b: Zig, Zag, Tag

Dandelion Readers

Book 6: Zip and Zap (Set 1 Units 1–10)

Book 6: Meg and the Bun (Set 2 Units 1–10)

Book 6: Top Dog (Set 3 Units 1-10)

Stage 7: x, y, ff, ll, ss, zz

LESSON RESOURCES

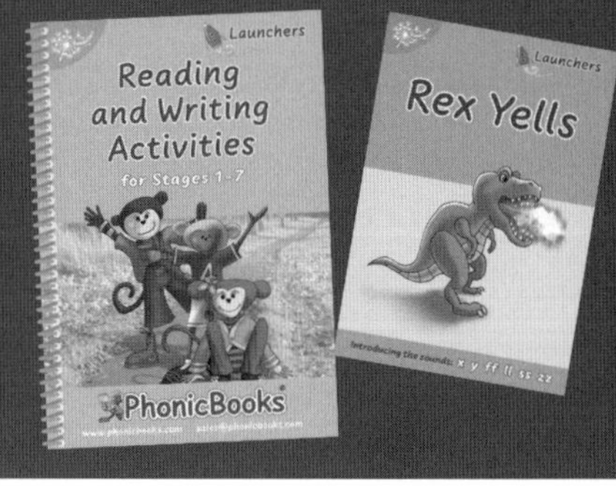

STEP 1
Preparation

20 mins

Reviewing sounds (3 mins)

- Using sound cards, review some of the previously learned sounds.

Learning goal (2 mins)

- Explain to the students that you will be teaching them to read and spell new words using the new sounds /x/ /y/ /ff/ /ll/ /ss/ /zz/ and the sounds they have previously learned.
- Introduce the book Dandelion Launchers Book 7a: Rex Yells.
- You will be completing some activities from Dandelion Launchers Stages 1–7 Activities.

Preparation (15 mins)

- Model the new focus sounds.
- Explain that the /x/ sound is two sounds: /k/ and /s/.
- When introducing double consonants, show the student a card with the digraph (e.g. 'ss').
- Explain that the two letters stand for one sound: this is an alternative way to spell the sound /s/.

Word building and blending

- First demonstrate how to build a word. Use only three sound cards, e.g. "boss."
- Draw three lines on the whiteboard, and tell the students that you are going to show them how to build the word "boss."
- As you say the word slowly, move your finger under the lines.
- Ask the students to listen to the first sound in the word "boss"—point to the first line. Emphasize the first sound as you say the whole word. The students respond—/b/.
- Then ask the students which letter spells the sound /b/. The students point to the letter (or you can tell them). Bring the letter down to the first line.

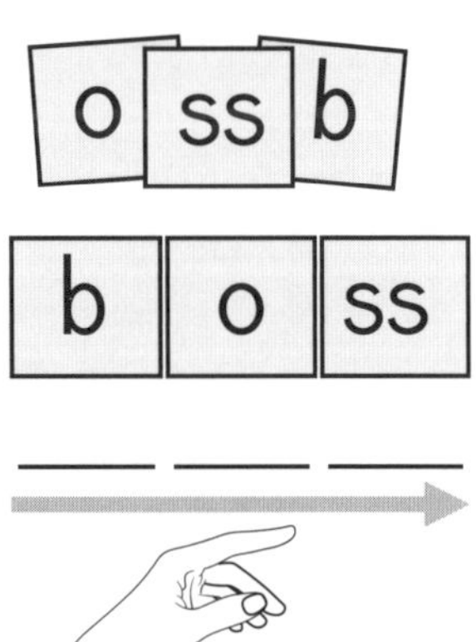

- Repeat with the second and last sounds in the word. Now ask the students to sound all three sounds and blend them into a word, moving your finger under the word: /b/ /o/ /ss/ → "boss."

Extension activities

1 Word reading

- Write the words you have created on the whiteboard. Then ask students to blend and read the words.
- Show how to say each sound individually and then blend them together to read the word. Model blending by pointing at each letter for segmenting and using a swishing motion with your finger for blending.

2 Oral segmenting

- Say a word aloud (e.g. "fix") and ask students to count the sounds in the word (3). Write the number of lines you need for all the sounds. Now ask students to listen to the sounds in the word and write a letter for every sound in the word as you spell the word.

3 Word chain

- Using sound cards, demonstrate how to build the word "fox."
- Say that you are going to change the word "fox" (moving your finger under the word) to "box." Ask the students to listen carefully to where the change has occurred. Move your finger under the word as you say it slowly. Once the change has been identified, invite a student to swap the sound card or letter. Ask all the students to sound out the word and read the new word, e.g. /f/ /o/ /x/ → "fox."
- Introduce the new sounds gradually. This allows students to incorporate the letters and sounds they have learned so far.
- Direct students through the following word-chain sequence: fox—box—boss—bess—bell—yell—till—tix—tox—box—fox

STEP 2
Application for reading
15 mins

Before reading (3 mins)

- Revisit the vocabulary taught in Step 1 (e.g. "bell"). Clearly say the word: /b/ /e/ /ll/
- Ask questions such as, "When do you ring a bell?"
- Then write the word on the whiteboard and refer back to it throughout the week for reinforcement.
- You could also draw a picture of a bicycle bell on the whiteboard or show an actual picture.

High-frequency words (2 mins)

- Pre-teach and reiterate these high-frequency words: "yells," "I," "the," "and," "was," "no," "be," "a," and "said."
- Explain that these are high-frequency words that have tricky spellings the students will learn later. Read each high-frequency word aloud. Write the words on the board, showing the separate graphemes in each word.

Application (10 mins)

- The chosen text for this reading activity is Book 7a: Rex Yells. Briefly introduce the book, its characters, and its context to spark interest and set the stage for engagement.
- Lead students through a directed reading of Book 7a: Rex Yells. Encourage students to sound out each word carefully and then blend the sounds together to form the word.
- Provide support by modeling the blending. This hands-on practice is crucial for reinforcing phonetic skills and building fluency.
- Encourage students to sound out each word and then blend to read. This is crucial for reinforcing their learning and for building their confidence.

Extension activities

- Following the initial reading, revisit Book 7a: Rex Yells with a focus on fluency.
- Reading the book again allows students to practice their newly acquired skills, this time with an emphasis on reading more smoothly and confidently.
- Create an interactive reading environment by inviting students to take turns reading aloud. Encourage them to point to each word as they read.
- As students read more fluently, support them to read with more expression and prosody.

STEP 3
Application for spelling
15 mins

Segmenting and spelling (5 mins)

- Ask students to complete the following: **Fill in the missing sounds** (Activities, page 147).
- Demonstrate correct pencil grip to the class. The pencil should rest comfortably between the thumb and index finger, supported by the middle finger, with the other two fingers curled inwards. The student should have their hands resting on the table and their feet planted squarely on the floor; the paper should be at a slight angle. The student should learn to move the pencil forward using their hand muscles.
- Distribute the **Fill in the missing sounds** activity to each student.
- Instruct students to look at each picture and use it to determine the missing sound in the corresponding word.
- Encourage the students to say the sounds as they write them and then blend the three sounds in each word together as they write them.
- After students complete the activity, individually model the formation of each letter that was filled in during the activity on the whiteboard. Focus on the starting point, stroke direction, and completion of each letter.

Sentence dictation (10 mins)

- Read out the dictation sentences (Activities, page 153): "Jill and Fuzz hid in the box." and "Rex was sad. Rex had no pal."
- Encourage the students to sound out the words as they spell them.

Extension activities

- Ask students to complete **Fill in all the missing sounds** (Activities, page 148) to practice writing whole words.
- Ask students to complete the **Matching lower to upper case game** (Activities, page 157) to match lower to upper case letters.
- Remind students how to segment the sounds in each word to spell them.
- For students who finish early or need additional practice with letter formation, provide extra activity sheets with different words or have them create their own "missing sound" examples using words from a word bank.
- Additionally, you can create your own sentences using the learned sounds and dictate them for the students to spell.

STEP 4
Comprehension and consolidation

15 mins

Book reading (5 mins)

- Reread Book 7a: Rex Yells.
- Revisiting the book helps to reinforce familiarity with the text and supports phonetic recognition and comprehension.

Sequencing (5 mins)

- For this activity, the students are going to retell the story, using the pictures and words in the **Retelling the story** activity (Activities, page 155).
- Divide students into small groups.
- Distribute the activity to each group.
- Decide whether to number the cards on the back to make sequencing easier for the students.
- Provide each group with a set of cards. Encourage collaboration as they work together to place the picture cards in the correct order of the story.
- Invite each group to retell the story using their arranged cards. Encourage them to use the word cards to narrate the story.
- Alternatively, after sequencing the story, the students can use the word cards to reinforce vocabulary. Ask students to match the word cards to the corresponding picture cards, promoting word recognition and comprehension.

Comprehension (5 mins)

- Check students have understood the story by completing the **Comprehension** activity (Activities, page 157).
- The aim of this activity is to reinforce vocabulary and story comprehension through a matching exercise.
- Distribute the activity to each student or small group.
- Cut out the words on the page. Then ask students to read and match them to the correct pictures.
- After matching, facilitate a discussion where students share their matches and explain their reasoning.

Extension activities

- Divide the class into pairs and give each pair a copy of the **Dice game** (Activities, page 163).
- Have students find and point to these words in Book 7a: Rex Yells: "Jill," "box," and "Fuzz."

STEP 5
Tracking progress

- Complete the **Bookmark** (Activities, page 162) to make a quick, formative assessment of students' progress.
- Hide the words and ask students to write them out as you read them, encouraging them to segment each sound.
- Then for a summative assessment of Stages 1–7, assign the **Reading Assessment** on page 59.

Extension activities

- Play the **Stepping stones game** (Activities, page 161).
- This game is suitable for 1–4 players and requires counters and a die.
- Students place their counters at the start of the stepping stones path. They then take turns rolling the die. They move their counter according to the number rolled.
- Upon landing on a stepping stone, the student reads the word or letter sound on that stone aloud.
- If a student lands on a stone with a directional arrow, they follow the arrow forward or backward.
- The first student to reach the end of the stepping stones path wins.
- Provide positive feedback and encouragement throughout the game.
- For those needing more support, help them to blend the letter sound or word with assistance.

PARALLEL BOOKS

In addition to Book 7a: Rex Yells, the following books also cover the focus sounds (/x/ /y/ /ff/ /ll/ /ss/ /zz/) and can be used for more practice of decoding, for book bags to take home.

Dandelion Launchers

Book 7b: Rex Will Not Sit

Dandelion Launchers Extras

Book 7a: Bob on the Sill

Book 7b: The Hill

Dandelion World

Book 7a: The Jazz Gig

Book 7b: In the Dell

Dandelion Readers

Book 7: Bob is Not Well (Set 1 Units 1–10)

Book 7: Up a Big Hill (Set 2 Units 1–10)

Book 7: I Will Sell (Set 3 Units 1–10)

LESSON PLANS

Stage 8: CVCC

LESSON RESOURCES

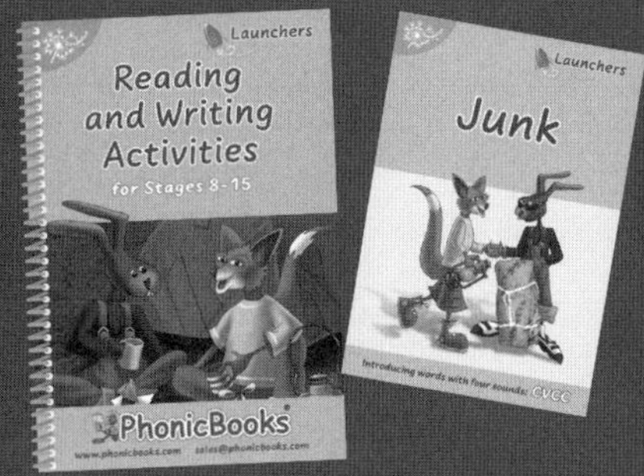

STEP 1
Preparation 15 mins

Learning goal (2 mins)

- Explain to the students that you will be teaching them to read and spell words with four sounds using the sounds they have previously learned.
- Introduce the book Dandelion Launchers Book 8a: Junk.
- You will be completing some activities from Dandelion Launchers Stages 8–15 Activities.

Word building and blending (13 mins)

- First demonstrate how to build a word. Use only four sound cards, e.g. for the word "sand."
- Draw four lines on the whiteboard, and tell the students that you are going to show them how to build the word "sand."
- As you say the word slowly, move your finger under the lines.
- Ask the students to listen to the first sound in the word "sand"—point to the first line. Emphasize the first sound as you say the whole word. The students respond—/s/.
- Then ask the students which letter spells the sound /s/. The students point to the letter (or you can tell them). Bring the letter down to the first line.
- Repeat with the remaining sounds in the word. Now ask the students to sound all four sounds and blend them into a word, moving your finger under the word: /s/ /a/ /n/ /d/ → "sand."
- The next time this is done, you can ask a student to participate and identify the sound and then letter and bring it down to the line.

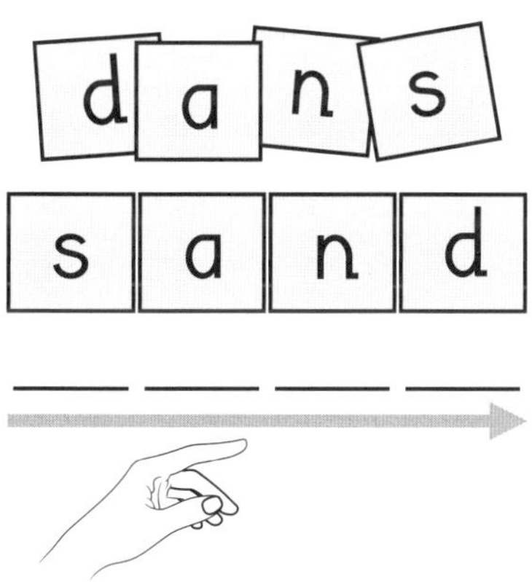

Extension activities

1 Word reading

- Write the words you have created on the whiteboard (if you haven't done so already). Then ask students to blend and read the words.
- Show how to say each sound individually and then blend them together to read the word. Model blending by using a swishing motion with your finger.
- Encourage students to follow your example with these words: "must," "tent," "hand," and "went."

2 Oral segmenting

- Say the word aloud (e.g. "mend") and count the sounds in the word (4). Write the number of lines you need for all the sounds. Now ask students to listen to the sounds in the word and write a letter for every sound in the word as you spell the word.

3 Word chain

- Using sound cards or magnetic letters, demonstrate how to build the word "tend." Explain to the students that you will be making one change to the word. They must be "sound detectives" and notice if you have added a sound, taken away a sound, or swapped a sound.
- Say that you are going to change the word "tend" (moving your finger under the word) to "tent." Ask the students to listen carefully to where the change has occurred. Move your finger under the word as you say it slowly. Once the change has been identified, invite a student to swap the sound card or letter. Ask all the students to sound out the word and read the new word, e.g. /t/ /e/ /n/ /t/ → "tent."
- Direct students through the following word-chain sequence: tend—tent—ten—tan—ban—band—hand—had—bad—bed—bend—tend

4 Reading game

- Play the game in Book 8a: Junk (pages 7–8) to familiarize students with the vocabulary in the book.

STEP 2
Application for reading
15 mins

Before reading (3 mins)

- Revisit the vocabulary taught in Step 1 (e.g. "tent"). Clearly say the word: /t/ /e/ /n/ /t/
- Then provide a simple definition such as, "A tent is a shelter made of canvas or nylon that you can use outside."
- Ask questions such as "When do you use a tent?" and "What rhymes with 'tent'?"
- Then write the word on the whiteboard and refer back to it throughout the week for reinforcement.
- You could also draw a picture of tent on the whiteboard or show an actual picture.

High-frequency words (2 mins)

- Pre-teach and reiterate these high-frequency words: "I," "of," "this," "old," "said," "to," "the," and "that."
- Explain that these are high-frequency words that have tricky spellings the students will learn later. Read each high-frequency word aloud. Write the words on the board, showing the separate graphemes in each word.

Application (10 mins)

- The chosen text for this reading activity is Book 8a: Junk. Briefly introduce the book, its characters, and its context to spark interest and set the stage for engagement.
- Lead students through a directed reading of Book 8a: Junk. Encourage students to sound out each word carefully and then blend the sounds together to form the word.
- Provide support by modeling the blending. This hands-on practice is crucial for reinforcing phonetic skills and building fluency.
- Encourage students to sound out each word and then blend to read. This is crucial for reinforcing their learning and for building their confidence.

Extension activities

- Following the initial reading, revisit Book 8a: Junk with a focus on fluency.
- Reading the book again allows students to practice their newly acquired skills.
- Create an interactive reading environment by inviting students to take turns reading aloud. Encourage them to point to each word as they read.
- As students read more fluently, support them to read with more expression and prosody.

STEP 3
Application for spelling
15 mins

Segmenting and spelling (5 mins)

- Ask students to complete the following: **Fill in the missing sounds** (Activities, page 9).
- Demonstrate correct pencil grip to the class. The pencil should rest comfortably between the thumb and index finger, supported by the middle finger, with the other two fingers curled inwards. The student should have their hands resting on the table and their feet planted squarely on the floor; the paper should be at a slight angle. The student should learn to move the pencil forward using their hand muscles.
- Distribute the **Fill in the missing sounds** activity to each student.
- Instruct students to look at each picture and use it to determine the missing sound in the corresponding word.
- Encourage the students to say the sounds as they write them and then blend the sounds in each word together as they write them.
- After students complete the activity, individually model the formation of each letter that was filled in during the activity on the whiteboard. Focus on the starting point, stroke direction, and completion of each letter.

Sentence dictation (10 mins)

- Read out the **Sentence dictation** sentences (Activities, page 13): "Alf went to the dump." and "Hank and Alf went off to camp."
- Encourage the students to sound out the words as they spell them.

Extension activities

- Ask students to complete **Fill in all the missing sounds** (Activities, page 10) to practice writing whole words.
- For students who finish early or need additional practice with letter formation, provide extra activity sheets with different words or have them create their own "missing sound" examples using words from a word bank.
- Additionally, you can create your own sentences using the learned sounds and dictate them for the students to spell.

STEP 4
Comprehension and consolidation

15 mins

Book reading (5 mins)

- Reread Book 8a: Junk.
- Revisiting the book helps to reinforce familiarity with the text and supports phonetic recognition and comprehension.

Sequencing (5 mins)

- For this activity, the students are going to retell the story, using the pictures and words in the **Retelling the story** activity (Activities, page 15).
- Divide students into small groups.
- Distribute the activity to each group.
- Decide whether to number the cards on the back to make sequencing easier for the students.
- Provide each group with a set of cards. Encourage collaboration as they work together to place the picture cards in the correct order of the story.
- Invite each group to retell the story using their arranged cards. Encourage them to use the word cards to narrate the story.
- Alternatively, after sequencing the story, the students can use the word cards to reinforce vocabulary. Ask students to match the word cards to the corresponding picture cards, promoting word recognition and comprehension.

Comprehension (5 mins)

- Check students have understood the story by completing the **Comprehension** activity (Activities, page 17).
- The aim of this activity is to reinforce vocabulary and story comprehension through a matching exercise.
- Distribute the activity to each student or small group.
- Cut out the words on the page. Then ask students to read and match them to the correct pictures.
- After matching, facilitate a discussion where students share their matches and explain their reasoning.

Extension activities

- Divide the class into pairs and give each pair a copy of the **Dice game** (Activities, page 23).
- Have students find and point to these words in Book 8a: Junk: "tent," "must," "went," and "mend."

STEP 5
Tracking progress

- Complete the **Bookmark** (Activities, page 22) to make a quick, formative assessment of students' progress.
- Hide the words and ask students to write them out as you read them, encouraging them to segment each sound.
- Depending on your findings, either revisit some of the activities to reinforce any specific skill gaps, or invite students to complete an extension activity.

Extension activities

- Complete the **Spelling assessment** for further assessment of students' progress (Activities, page 26)
- Play the **Stepping stones game** (Activities, page 21).
- This game is suitable for 1–4 players and requires counters and a die.
- Students place their counters at the start of the stepping stones path. They then take turns rolling the die. They move their counter according to the number rolled.
- Upon landing on a stepping stone, the student reads the word on that stone aloud.
- If a student lands on a stone with a directional arrow, they follow the arrow forward or backward.
- The first student to reach the end of the stepping stones path wins.
- For those needing more support, help them to blend the letter sound or word with assistance.

PARALLEL BOOKS

In addition to Book 8a: Junk, the following books also cover CVCC words and can be used for more practice of decoding, for book bags to take home.

Dandelion Launchers

Book 8b: The Gift

Dandelion Launchers Extras

Book 8a: Lost

Book 8b: Jump!

Dandelion World

Book 8a: Kids at Camp

Book 8b: At Dusk

Dandelion Readers

Book 8: The Lost Box (Set 1 Units 1–10)

Book 8: Lost in the Pond (Set 2 Units 1–10)

Book 8: The Best Gift (Set 3 Units 1–10)

LESSON PLANS

Stage 9: CCVC

STEP 1
Preparation

20 mins

Reviewing sounds (5 mins)

- Using sound cards or a whiteboard, review some previously learned CVCC words.

Learning goal (2 mins)

- Explain to the students that you will be teaching them to read and spell words with four sounds using the sounds they have previously learned.
- Introduce the book Dandelion Launchers Book 9a: Don't Spill.
- You will be completing some activities from Dandelion Launchers Stages 8–15 Activities.

Word building and blending (15 mins)

- First demonstrate how to build a word. Use only four sound cards, e.g. for the word "step."
- Draw four lines on the whiteboard, and tell the students that you are going to show them how to build the word "step."
- As you say the word slowly, move your finger under the lines.
- Ask the students to listen to the first sound in the word "step"—point to the first line. Emphasize the first sound as you say the whole word. The students respond—/s/.
- Then ask the students which letter spells the sound /s/. The students point to the letter (or you can tell them). Bring the letter down to the first line.
- Repeat with the remaining sounds in the word. Now ask the students to sound all four sounds and blend them into a word, moving your finger under the word: /s/ /t/ /e/ /p/ → "step."
- The next time this is done, you can ask a student to participate and identify the sound and then letter and bring it down to the line.

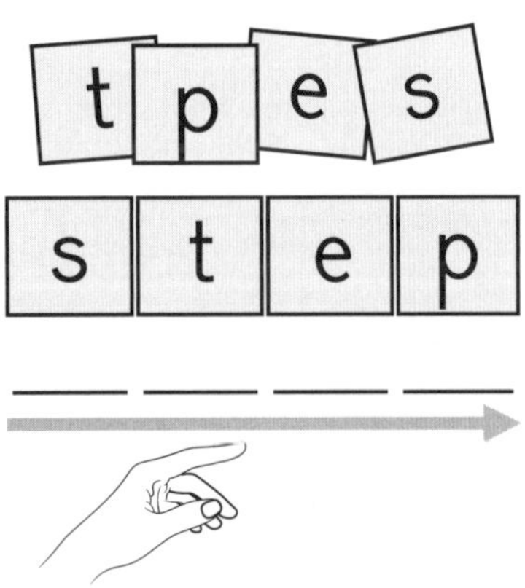

LESSON RESOURCES

Extension activities

1 Word reading

- Write the words you have created on the whiteboard (if you haven't done so already). Then ask students to blend and read the words.
- Show how to say each sound individually and then blend them together to read the word. Model blending by using a swishing motion with your finger.
- Encourage students to follow your example with these words: "step," "frog," "sled," and "grab."

2 Oral segmenting

- Say the word aloud (e.g. "spot") and count the sounds in the word (4). Write the number of lines you need for all the sounds. Now ask students to listen to the sounds in the word and write a letter for every sound in the word as you spell the word.

3 Word chain

- Using sound cards or magnetic letters, demonstrate how to build the word "slot." Explain to the students that you will be making one change to the word. They must be "sound detectives" and notice if you have added a sound, taken away a sound, or swapped a sound.
- Say that you are going to change the word "slot" (moving your finger under the word) to "slat." Ask the students to listen carefully to where the change has occurred. Move your finger under the words as you say it slowly. Once the change has been identified, invite a student to swap the sound card or letter. Ask all the students to sound out the word and read the new word, e.g. /s/ /l/ /a/ /t/ → "slat."
- Direct students through the following word-chain sequence: slot—slat—slap—lap—clap—cap—camp—lamp—limp—lip—slip—slop—slot

STEP 2
Application for reading

15 mins

Before reading (3 mins)

- Pre-teach difficult vocabulary in the book (e.g. "glum" and "brim"). Clearly say the word: /g/ /l/ /u/ /m/
- Then provide a simple definition, e.g. "Glum describes a feeling of sadness."
- Ask questions such as "Can you think of a book where a character felt glum?"
- Then write the word on the whiteboard and refer back to it throughout the week for reinforcement.

High-frequency words (2 mins)

- Pre-teach and reiterate these high-frequency words: "have," "a," "of," "don't," "says," "the," "to," and "is."
- Explain that these are high-frequency words that have tricky spellings the students will learn later. Read each high-frequency word aloud. Write the words on the board, showing the separate graphemes in each word.

Application (10 mins)

- The chosen text for this reading activity is Book 9a: Don't Spill. Briefly introduce the book, its characters, and its context to spark interest and set the stage for engagement.
- Lead students through a directed reading of Book 9a: Don't Spill. Encourage students to sound out each word carefully and then blend the sounds together to form the word.
- Provide support by modeling the blending. This hands-on practice is crucial for reinforcing phonetic skills and building fluency.
- Encourage students to sound out each word and then blend to read. This is crucial for reinforcing their learning and for building their confidence.

Extension activities

- Following the initial reading, revisit Book 9a: Don't Spill with a focus on fluency.
- Reading the book again allows students to practice their newly acquired skills, this time with an emphasis on reading more smoothly and confidently.
- Create an interactive reading environment by inviting students to take turns reading aloud. Encourage them to point to each word as they read.
- As students read more fluently, support them to read with more expression and prosody.

STEP 3
Application for spelling

15 mins

Segmenting and spelling (5 mins)

- Ask students to complete the following: **Fill in the missing sounds** (Activities, page 31).
- Demonstrate correct pencil grip to the class. The pencil should rest comfortably between the thumb and index finger, supported by the middle finger, with the other two fingers curled inwards. The student should have their hands resting on the table and their feet planted squarely on the floor; the paper should be at a slight angle. The student should learn to move the pencil forward using their hand muscles.
- Distribute the **Fill in the missing sounds** activity to each student.
- Instruct students to look at each picture and use it to determine the missing sound in the corresponding word.
- Encourage the students to say the sounds as they write them and then blend the sounds in each word together as they write them.
- After students complete the activity, individually model the formation of each letter that was filled in during the activity on the whiteboard. Focus on the starting point, stroke direction, and completion of each letter.

Sentence dictation (10 mins)

- Read out the **Sentence dictation** sentences (Activities, page 35): "Viv fills the cups to the brim." and "Viv and Fred trip and spill the milk."
- Encourage the students to sound out the words as they spell them.

Extension activities

- Ask students to complete **Fill in all the missing sounds** (Activities, page 32) to practice writing whole words.
- For students who finish early or need additional practice with letter formation, provide extra activity sheets with different words or have them create their own "missing sound" examples using words from a word bank.
- Additionally, you can create your own sentences using the learned sounds and dictate them for the students to spell.

STEP 4
Comprehension and consolidation

15 mins

Book reading (5 mins)

- Reread Book 9a: Don't Spill.
- Revisiting the book helps to reinforce familiarity with the text and supports phonetic recognition and comprehension.

Sequencing (5 mins)

- For this activity, the students are going to retell the story, using the pictures and words in the **Retelling the story** activity (Activities, page 37).
- Divide students into small groups.
- Distribute the activity to each group.
- Decide whether to number the cards on the back to make sequencing easier for the students.
- Provide each group with a set of cards. Encourage collaboration as they work together to place the picture cards in the correct order of the story.
- Invite each group to retell the story using their arranged cards. Encourage them to use the word cards to narrate the story.
- Alternatively, after sequencing the story, the students can use the word cards to reinforce vocabulary. Ask students to match the word cards to the corresponding picture cards, promoting word recognition and comprehension.

Comprehension (5 mins)

- Check students have understood the story by completing the **Comprehension** activity (Activities, page 39).
- The aim of this activity is to reinforce vocabulary and story comprehension through a matching exercise.
- Distribute the activity to each student or small group.
- Cut out the words on the page. Then ask students to read and match them to the correct pictures.
- After matching, facilitate a discussion where students share their matches and explain their reasoning.

Extension activities

- Divide the class into pairs and give each pair a copy of the **Dice game** (Activities, page 45).
- Have students find and point to these words in Book 9a: Don't Spill: "brim," "drip," and "glum."

STEP 5
Tracking progress

- Complete the **Bookmark** (Activities, page 44) to make a quick, formative assessment of students' progress.
- Hide the words and ask students to write them out as you read them, encouraging them to segment each sound.
- Depending on your findings, either revisit some of the activities to reinforce any specific skill gaps, or invite students to complete an extension activity.

Extension activities

- Complete the **Spelling assessment** for further assessment of students' progress (Activities, page 48)
- Play the **Stepping stones game** (Activities, page 43).
- This game is suitable for 1–4 players and requires counters and a die.
- Students place their counters at the start of the stepping stones path. They then take turns rolling the die. They move their counter according to the number rolled.
- Upon landing on a stepping stone, the student reads the word on that stone aloud.
- If a student lands on a stone with a directional arrow, they follow the arrow forwards or backwards.
- The first student to reach the end of the stepping stones path wins.
- For those needing more support, help them to blend the letter sound or word with assistance.

PARALLEL BOOKS

In addition to Book 9a: Don't Spill, the following books also cover CCVC words and can be used for more practice of decoding, for book bags to take home.

Dandelion Launchers

Book 9b: Floss

Dandelion Launchers Extras

Book 9a: Bob is Glum

Book 9b: Stop the Pram!

Dandelion World

Book 9a: Up the Cliff!

Book 9b: Clam, Crab, Gull

Dandelion Readers

Book 9: Flip and Flop Slip (Set 1)

Book 9: The Trap (Set 2)

Book 9: Fred Has a Plan (Set 3)

LESSON PLANS

Stage 10: CCVCC

STEP 1
Preparation 20 mins

Reviewing sounds (3 mins)

- Using sound cards or a whiteboard, review some previously learned CCVC words.

Learning goal (2 mins)

- Explain to the students that you will be teaching them to read and spell words with five sounds using the sounds they have previously learned.
- Introduce the book Dandelion Launchers Book 10a: Stunt Rat.
- You will be completing some activities from Dandelion Launchers Stages 8–15 Activities.

Word building and blending (15 mins)

- First demonstrate how to build a word. Use only five sound cards, e.g. for the word "drink."
- Draw five lines on the whiteboard, and tell the students that you are going to show them how to build the word "drink."
- As you say the word slowly, move your finger under the lines.
- Ask the students to listen to the first sound in the word "drink"—point to the first line. Emphasize the first sound as you say the whole word. The students respond—/d/.
- Then ask the students which letter spells the sound /d/. The students point to the letter (or you can tell them). Bring the letter down to the first line.
- Repeat with the remaining sounds in the word. Now ask the students to sound all five sounds and blend them into a word, moving your finger under the word: /d/ /r/ /i/ /n/ /k/ → "drink."
- The next time this is done, you can ask a student to participate and identify the sound and then letter and bring it down to the line.

LESSON RESOURCES

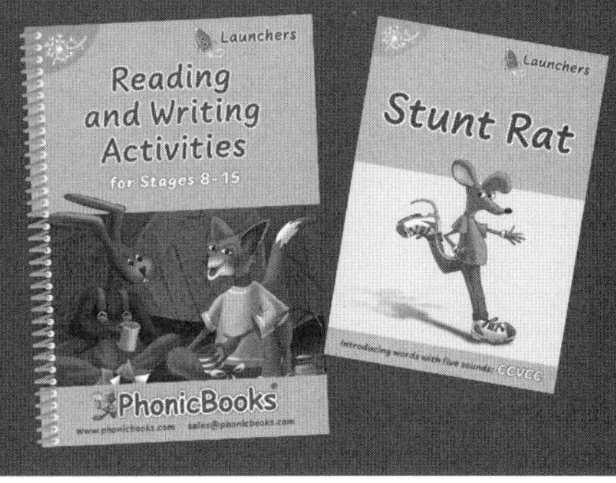

Extension activities

1 Word reading

- Write the words you have created on the whiteboard. Then ask students to blend and read the words.
- Show how to say each sound individually and then blend them together to read the word. Model blending by using a swishing motion with your finger.
- Encourage students to follow your example with these words: "drink," "stamp," and "trunk."

2 Oral segmenting

- Say the word aloud (e.g. "glint") and count the sounds in the word (5). Write the number of lines you need for all the sounds. Now ask students to listen to the sounds in the word and write a letter for every sound in the word as you spell the word.

3 Word chain

- Using letter cards or magnetic letters, demonstrate how to build the word "brand." Explain to the students that you will be making one change to the word. They must be "sound detectives" and notice if you have added a sound, taken away a sound, or swapped a sound.
- Say that you are going to change the word "brand" (moving your finger under the word) to "bland." Ask the students to listen carefully to where the change has occurred. Move your finger under the words as you say it slowly. Once the change has been identified, invite a student to swap the letter card or letter. Ask all the students to sound out the word and read the new word, e.g. /b/ /l/ /a/ /n/ /d/ → "bland."
- Introduce the new sounds gradually. This allows students to incorporate the letters and sounds they have learned so far.
- Direct students through the following word-chain sequence: brand—bland—land—sand—stand—stan—clan—clam—clamp—cramp—cram—ram—ran—bran—brand

STEP 2
Application for reading
15 mins

Before reading (3 mins)

- Revisit the vocabulary taught in Step 1 (e.g. "stunt"). Clearly say the word: /s/ /t/ /u/ /n/ /t/.
- Then provide a simple definition, e.g. "A stunt is an action that shows skill or bravery."
- Ask questions such as "What rhymes with stunt?" and "Who performs stunts?"
- Then write the word on the whiteboard and refer back to it throughout the week for reinforcement.
- You could also draw a picture of a character performing a stunt on a bike or skateboard on the whiteboard or show an actual picture.

High-frequency words (2 mins)

- Pre-teach and reiterate these high-frequency words: he," "as," "I," "be," "a," "says," and "the."
- Explain that these are high-frequency words that have tricky spellings the students will learn later. Read each high-frequency word aloud. Write the words on the board, showing the separate graphemes in each word.

Application (10 mins)

- The chosen text for this reading activity is Book 10a: Stunt Rat. Briefly introduce the book, its characters, and its context to spark interest and set the stage for engagement.
- Lead students through a directed reading of Book 10a: Stunt Rat. Encourage students to sound out each word carefully and then blend the sounds together to form the word.
- Provide support by modeling the blending. This hands-on practice is crucial for reinforcing phonetic skills and building fluency.
- Encourage students to sound out each word and then blend to read. This is crucial for reinforcing their learning and for building their confidence.

Extension activities

- Following the initial reading, revisit Book 10a: Stunt Rat with a focus on fluency.
- Reading the book again allows students to practice their newly acquired skills.
- Create an interactive reading environment by inviting students to take turns reading aloud. Encourage them to point to each word as they read.
- As students read more fluently, support them to read with more expression and prosody.

STEP 3
Application for spelling
15 mins

Segmenting and spelling (5 mins)

- Ask students to complete the following: **Fill in the missing sounds** (Activities, page 53).
- Demonstrate correct pencil grip to the class. The pencil should rest comfortably between the thumb and index finger, supported by the middle finger, with the other two fingers curled inwards. The student should have their hands resting on the table and their feet planted squarely on the floor; the paper should be at a slight angle. The student should learn to move the pencil forward using their hand muscles.
- Distribute the **Fill in the missing sounds** activity to each student.
- Instruct students to look at each picture and use it to determine the missing sound in the corresponding word.
- Encourage the students to say the sounds as they write them and then blend the sounds in each word together as they write them.
- After students complete the activity, individually model the formation of each letter that was filled in during the activity on the whiteboard. Focus on the starting point, stroke direction, and completion of each letter.

Sentence dictation (10 mins)

- Read out the **Sentence dictation** sentences (Activities, page 57): "Ken lifts up the twigs." and "Ken springs off and Bob pants."
- Encourage the students to sound out the words as they spell them.

Extension activities

- Ask students to complete **Fill in all the missing sounds** (Activities, page 54) to practice writing whole words.
- For students who finish early or need additional practice with letter formation, provide extra activity sheets with different words or have them create their own "missing sound" examples using words from a word bank.
- Additionally, you can create your own sentences using the learned sounds and dictate them for the students to spell.

STEP 4
Comprehension and consolidation
15 mins

Book reading (5 mins)

- Reread Book 10a: Stunt Rat.
- Revisiting the book helps to reinforce familiarity with the text and supports phonetic recognition and comprehension.

Sequencing (5 mins)

- For this activity, the students are going to retell the story, using the pictures and words in the **Retelling the story** activity (Activities, page 59).
- Divide students into small groups.
- Distribute the activity to each group.
- Decide whether to number the cards on the back to make sequencing easier for the students.
- Provide each group with a set of cards. Encourage collaboration as they work together to place the picture cards in the correct order of the story.
- Invite each group to retell the story using their arranged cards. Encourage them to use the word cards to narrate the story.
- Alternatively, after sequencing the story, the students can use the word cards to reinforce vocabulary. Ask students to match the word cards to the corresponding picture cards, promoting word recognition and comprehension.

Comprehension (5 mins)

- Check students have understood the story by completing the **Comprehension** activity (Activities, page 61).
- The aim of this activity is to reinforce vocabulary and story comprehension through a matching exercise.
- Distribute the activity to each student or small group.
- Cut out the words on the page. Then ask students to read and match them to the correct pictures.
- After matching, facilitate a discussion where students share their matches and explain their reasoning.

Extension activities

- Divide the class into pairs and give each pair a copy of the **Dice game** (Activities, page 67).
- Have students find and point to these words in Book 10a: Stunt Rat: "stunt" and "swims."

STEP 5
Tracking progress

- Complete the **Bookmark** (Activities, page 66) to make a quick, formative assessment of students' progress.
- Hide the words and ask students to write them out as you read them, encouraging them to segment each sound.
- Then for a summative assessment of Stages 8–10, assign the **Reading Assessment** on page 67.

Extension activities

- Complete the **Spelling assessment** for further assessment of students' progress (Activities, page 70)
- Play the **Stepping stones game** (Activities, page 65).
- This game is suitable for 1–4 players and requires counters and a die.
- Students place their counters at the start of the stepping stones path. They then take turns rolling the die. They move their counter according to the number rolled.
- Upon landing on a stepping stone, the student reads the word on that stone aloud.
- If a student lands on a stone with a directional arrow, they follow the arrow forward or backward.
- The first student to reach the end of the stepping stones path wins.

PARALLEL BOOKS

In addition to Book 10a: Stunt Rat, the following books also cover CCVCC words and can be used for more practice of decoding, for book bags to take home.

Dandelion Launchers

Book 10b: Frank Swims

Dandelion Launchers Extras

Book 10a: Punk Smells Crisp Chips

Book 10b: Mom Gets Strict

Dandelion World

Book 10a: Frost Melts

Book 10b: Frank and the Skunk

Dandelion Readers

Book 10: The Stink (Set 1 Units 1–10)

Book 10: Punk and the Plums (Set 2 Units 1–10)

Book 10: The Stilts (Set 3 Units 1–10)

Stage 11: ch

STEP 1
Preparation

20 mins

Reviewing sounds (3 mins)

- Using sound cards or a whiteboard, review some previously learned CCVCC words.

Learning goal (2 mins)

- Explain to the students that you will be teaching them to read and spell words using the consonant digraph /ch/ and sounds they have previously learned.
- Introduce the book Dandelion Launchers Book 11a: Nuts for Lunch.
- You will be completing some activities from Dandelion Launchers Stages 8–15 Activities.

Preparation (15 mins)

- Introduce and model the new focus sound: /ch/.

Word building and blending

- First demonstrate how to build a word. Use only three sound cards, e.g. for the word "chip."
- Draw three lines on the whiteboard, and tell the students that you are going to show them how to build the word "chip."
- As you say the word slowly, move your finger under the lines.
- Ask the students to listen to the first sound in the word "chip"—point to the first line. Emphasize the first sound as you say the whole word. The students respond—/ch/.
- Then ask the students which letters spell the sound /ch/. Remind students that two letters 'c' and 'h' spell the sound /ch/. Bring the letters down to the first line.
- Repeat with the second and last sounds in the word. Now ask the students to sound all three sounds and blend them into a word, moving your finger under the word: /ch/ /i/ /p/ → "chip."

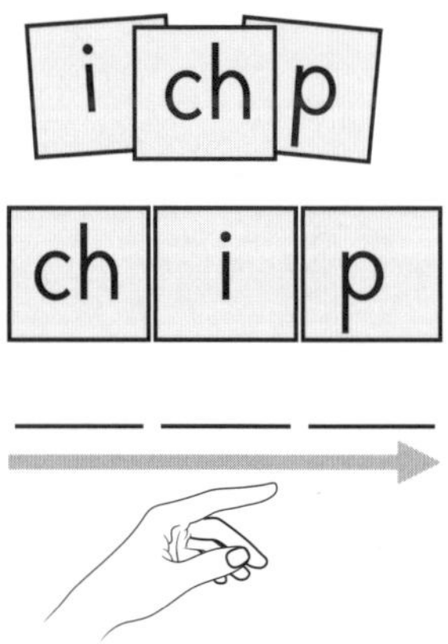

LESSON RESOURCES

Extension activities

1 Word reading

- Write the words you have created on the whiteboard (if you haven't done so already). Then ask students to blend and read the words.
- Show how to say each sound individually and then blend them together to read the word. Model blending by using a swishing motion with your finger.
- Encourage students to follow your example with these words: "chest," "lunch," "bench," and "munch."

2 Oral segmenting

- Say a word aloud (e.g. "munch") and ask students to listen to the sounds in the word (4). Students then spell the word sound by sound. This is important as it links reading and spelling.

3 Word chain

- Using sound cards or magnetic letters, demonstrate how to build the word "lunch." Explain to the students that you will be making one change to the word. They must be "sound detectives" and notice if you have added a sound, taken away a sound, or swapped a sound.
- Say that you are going to change the word "lunch" (moving your finger under the word) to "munch." Ask the students to listen carefully to where the change has occurred. Move your finger under the word as you say it slowly. Once the change has been identified, invite a student to swap the sound card or letter. Ask all the students to sound out the word and read the new word, e.g, /m/ /u/ /n/ /ch/ → "munch."
- Direct students through the following word-chain sequence: lunch—munch—punch—bunch—hunch—lunch

STEP 2
Application for reading

15 mins

Before reading (3 mins)

- Revisit the vocabulary taught in Step 1 (e.g. "lunch"). Clearly say the word: /l / /u/ /n/ /ch/
- Then provide a simple definition, e.g. "Lunch is a meal eaten in the middle of the day."
- Ask questions such as "What do you eat for lunch?" and "What do squirrels eat?"
- Then write the word on the whiteboard and refer back to it throughout the week for reinforcement.
- You could also draw a picture of someone eating lunch on the whiteboard or show an actual picture.

High-frequency words (2 mins)

- Pre-teach and reiterate these high-frequency words: "a," "was," "to," "the," "for," "his," "I," "have," "said," "plant," and "off."
- Explain that these are high-frequency words that have tricky spellings the students will learn later. Read each high-frequency word aloud. Write the words on the board, showing the separate graphemes in each word.

Application (10 mins)

- The chosen text for this reading activity is Book 11a: Nuts for Lunch. Briefly introduce the book, its characters, and its context to spark interest and set the stage for engagement.
- Lead students through a directed reading of Book 11a: Nuts for Lunch. Encourage students to sound out each word carefully and then blend the sounds together to form the word.
- Provide support by modeling the blending. This hands-on practice is crucial for reinforcing phonetic skills and building fluency.
- Encourage students to sound out each word and then blend to read. This is crucial for reinforcing their learning and for building their confidence.

Extension activities

- Following the initial reading, revisit Book 11a: Nuts for Lunch with a focus on fluency.
- Reading the book again allows students to practice their newly acquired skills.
- Create an interactive reading environment by inviting students to take turns reading aloud. Encourage them to point to each word as they read.
- As students read more fluently, support them to read with more expression and prosody.

STEP 3
Application for spelling

15 mins

Segmenting and spelling (5 mins)

- Ask students to complete the following: **Fill in the ch sound** (Activities, page 75).
- Demonstrate correct pencil grip to the class. The pencil should rest comfortably between the thumb and index finger, supported by the middle finger, with the other two fingers curled inwards. The student should have their hands resting on the table and their feet planted squarely on the floor; the paper should be at a slight angle. The student should learn to move the pencil forward using their hand muscles.
- Distribute the **Fill in the missing sounds** activity to each student.
- Instruct students to look at each picture and use it to determine the missing sound in the corresponding word.
- Encourage the students to say the sounds as they write them and then blend the sounds in each word together as they write them.
- After students complete the activity, individually model the formation of each letter that was filled in during the activity on the whiteboard. Focus on the starting point, stroke direction, and completion of each letter.

Sentence dictation (10 mins)

- Read out the **Sentence dictation** sentences (Activities, page 79): "I have nuts to munch." and "Let's plant a nut next to the bench."
- Encourage the students to sound out the words as they spell them.

Extension activities

- Ask students to complete **Fill in all the missing sounds** (Activities, page 76) to practice writing whole words
- For students who finish early or need additional practice with letter formation, provide extra activity sheets with different words or have them create their own "missing sound" examples using words from a word bank.
- Additionally, you can create your own sentences using the learned sounds and dictate them for the students to spell.

STEP 4
Comprehension and consolidation

15 mins

Book reading (5 mins)

- Reread Book 11a: Nuts for Lunch.
- Revisiting the book helps to reinforce familiarity with the text and supports phonetic recognition and comprehension.

Sequencing (5 mins)

- For this activity, the students are going to retell the story, using the pictures and words in the **Retelling the story** activity (Activities, page 81).
- Divide students into small groups.
- Distribute the activity to each group.
- Decide whether to number the cards on the back to make sequencing easier for the students.
- Provide each group with a set of cards. Encourage collaboration as they work together to place the picture cards in the correct order of the story.
- Invite each group to retell the story using their arranged cards. Encourage them to use the word cards to narrate the story.
- Alternatively, after sequencing the story, the students can use the word cards to reinforce vocabulary. Ask students to match the word cards to the corresponding picture cards, promoting word recognition and comprehension.

Comprehension (5 mins)

- Check students have understood the story by completing the **Comprehension** activity (Activities, page 83).
- The aim of this activity is to reinforce vocabulary and story comprehension through a matching exercise.
- Distribute the page to each student or small group.
- Cut out the words on the page. Then ask students to read and match them to the correct pictures.
- After matching, facilitate a discussion where students share their matches and explain their reasoning.

Extension activities

- Divide the class into pairs and give each pair a copy of the **Dice game** (Activities, page 89).
- Have students find and point to these words in Book 11a: Nuts for Lunch: "lunch," "bench," "munch," and "chest."

STEP 5
Tracking progress

- Complete the **Bookmark** (Activities, page 88) to make a quick, formative assessment of students' progress.
- Hide the words and ask students to write them out as you read them, encouraging them to segment each sound.
- Depending on your findings, either revisit some of the activities to reinforce any specific skill gaps, or invite students to complete an extension activity.

Extension activities

- Complete the **Spelling assessment** for further assessment of students' progress (Activities, page 92)
- Play the **Stepping stones game** (Activities, page 87).
- This game is suitable for 1–4 players and requires counters and a die.
- Students place their counters at the start of the stepping stones path. They then take turns rolling the die. They move their counter according to the number rolled.
- Upon landing on a stepping stone, the student reads the word on that stone aloud.
- If a student lands on a stone with a directional arrow, they follow the arrow forward or backward.
- The first student to reach the end of the stepping stones path wins.
- For those needing more support, help them to blend the letter sound or word with assistance.

PARALLEL BOOKS

In addition to Book 11a: Nuts for Lunch, the following books also cover the /ch/ sound and can be used for more practice of decoding, for book bags to take home.

Dandelion Launchers

Book 11b: The Champ

Dandelion Launchers Extras

Book 11a: The Big Chip

Book 11b: Chit Chat

Dandelion World

Book 11a: Crunch, Munch!

Book 11b: Chimp Chums

Dandelion Readers

Book 11: Pip Gets Rich (Set 1 Units 11–20)

Book 11: Twin Chimps (Set 2 Units 11–20)

LESSON PLANS

Stage 12: sh

STEP 1 Preparation

20 mins

Reviewing sounds (3 mins)

- Using sound cards or a whiteboard, review some previously learned words containing the /ch/ sound.

Learning goal (2 mins)

- Explain to the students that you will be teaching them to read and spell words using the consonant digraph /sh/ and sounds they have previously learned.
- Introduce the book Dandelion Launchers Book 12a: Shep and Tosh.
- You will be completing some activities from Dandelion Launchers Stages 8–15 Activities.

Preparation (15 mins)

- Introduce and model the new focus sound: /sh/.

Word building and blending

- First demonstrate how to build a word. Use only three sound cards, e.g. for the word "ship."
- Draw three lines on the whiteboard, and tell the students that you are going to show them how to build the word "ship."
- As you say the word slowly, move your finger under the lines.
- Ask the students to listen to the first sound in the word "ship"—point to the first line. Emphasize the first sound as you say the whole word. The students respond—/sh/.
- Then ask the students which letters spell the sound /sh/. Remind students that two letters 's' and 'h' spell the sound /sh/. Bring the letters down to the first line.
- Repeat with the second and last sounds in the word. Now ask the students to sound all three sounds and blend them into a word, moving your finger under the word: /sh/ /i/ /p/ → "ship"

LESSON RESOURCES

Extension activities

1. **Word reading**
   - Write the words you have created on the whiteboard (if you haven't done so already). Then ask students to blend and read the words.
   - Show how to say each sound individually and then blend them together to read the word. Model blending by using a swishing motion with your finger.
   - Encourage students to follow your example with these words: "wish" and "shrub."

2. **Oral segmenting**
   - Say a word aloud (e.g. "wish") and ask students to listen to the sounds in the word (3). Students then spell the word sound by sound. This is important as it links reading and spelling.

3. **Word chain**
   - Using sound cards or magnetic letters, demonstrate how to build the word "wish." Explain to the students that you will be making one change to the word. They must be "sound detectives" and notice if you have added a sound, taken away a sound, or swapped a sound.
   - Say that you are going to change the word "wish" (moving your finger under the word) to "dish." Ask the students to listen carefully to where the change has occurred. Move your finger under the words as you say it slowly. Once the change has been identified, invite a student to swap the sound card or letter. Ask all the students to sound out the word and read the new word, e.g. /d/ /i/ /sh/ → "dish."
   - Direct students through the following word-chain sequence: wish—dish—dash—ash—cash—clash—flash—flush—lush—blush—brush—rush—mush—mash—dash—dish—wish

STEP 2
Application for reading
15 mins

Before reading (3 mins)

- Pre-teach difficult vocabulary in the book (e.g. "shrub"). Clearly say the word: /sh/ /r/ /u/ /b/.
- Then provide a simple definition, e.g. "A shrub is a type of small, woody plant."
- Ask questions such as "Can you name a type of shrub you know?"
- Then write the word on the whiteboard and refer back to it throughout the week for reinforcement.
- You could also draw a picture of a shrub on the whiteboard or show an actual picture.

High-frequency words (2 mins)

- Pre-teach and reiterate these high-frequency words: "I," "a," "was," "you," "be," "my," "to," "no," "yelled," and "said."
- Explain that these are high-frequency words that have tricky spellings the students will learn later. Read each high-frequency word aloud. Write the words on the board, showing the separate graphemes in each word.

Application (10 mins)

- The chosen text for this reading activity is Book 12a: Shep and Tosh. Briefly introduce the book, its characters, and its context to spark interest and set the stage for engagement.
- Lead students through a directed reading of Book 12a: Shep and Tosh. Encourage students to sound out each word carefully and then blend the sounds together to form the word.
- Provide support by modeling the blending. This hands-on practice is crucial for reinforcing phonetic skills and building fluency.
- Encourage students to sound out each word and then blend to read. This is crucial for reinforcing their learning and for building their confidence.

Extension activities

- Following the initial reading, revisit Book 12a: Shep and Tosh with a focus on fluency.
- Reading the book again allows students to practice their newly acquired skills.
- Create an interactive reading environment by inviting students to take turns reading aloud. Encourage them to point to each word as they read.
- As students read more fluently, support them to read with more expression and prosody.

STEP 3
Application for spelling
15 mins

Segmenting and spelling (5 mins)

- Ask students to complete the following: **Fill in the sh sound** (Activities, page 97).
- Demonstrate correct pencil grip to the class. The pencil should rest comfortably between the thumb and index finger, supported by the middle finger, with the other two fingers curled inwards. The student should have their hands resting on the table and their feet planted squarely on the floor; the paper should be at a slight angle. The student should learn to move the pencil forward using their hand muscles.
- Distribute the **Fill in the missing sounds** activity to each student.
- Instruct students to look at each picture and use it to determine the missing sound in the corresponding word.
- Encourage the students to say the sounds as they write them and then blend the sounds in each word together as they write them.
- After students complete the activity, individually model the formation of each letter that was filled in during the activity on the whiteboard. Focus on the starting point, stroke direction, and completion of each letter.

Sentence dictation (10 mins)

- Read out the **Sentence dictation** sentences (Activities, page 101): "The big dog yelled at Shep." and "Shep ran and hid in a shrub."
- Encourage the students to sound out the words as they spell them.

Extension activities

- Ask students to complete **Fill in all the missing sounds** (Activities, page 98) to practice writing whole words.
- For students who finish early or need additional practice with letter formation, provide extra activity sheets with different words or have them create their own "missing sound" examples using words from a word bank.
- Additionally, you can create your own sentences using the learned sounds and dictate them for the students to spell.

STEP 4
Comprehension and consolidation

15 mins

Book reading (5 mins)

- Reread Book 12a: Shep and Tosh.
- Revisiting the book helps to reinforce familiarity with the text and supports phonetic recognition and comprehension.

Sequencing (5 mins)

- For this activity, the students are going to retell the story, using the pictures and words in the **Retelling the story** activity (Activities, page 103).
- Divide students into small groups.
- Distribute the activity to each group.
- Decide whether to number the cards on the back to make sequencing easier for the students.
- Provide each group with a set of cards. Encourage collaboration as they work together to place the picture cards in the correct order of the story.
- Invite each group to retell the story using their arranged cards. Encourage them to use the word cards to narrate the story.
- Alternatively, after sequencing the story, the students can use the word cards to reinforce vocabulary. Ask students to match the word cards to the corresponding picture cards, promoting word recognition and comprehension.

Comprehension (5 mins)

- Check students have understood the story by completing the **Comprehension** activity (Activities, page 105).
- The aim of this activity is to reinforce vocabulary and story comprehension through a matching exercise.
- Distribute the activity to each student or small group.
- Cut out the words on the page. Then ask students to read and match them to the correct pictures.
- After matching, facilitate a discussion where students share their matches and explain their reasoning.

Extension activities

- Divide the class into pairs and give each pair a copy of the **Dice game** (Activities, page 111).

STEP 5
Tracking progress

- Complete the **Bookmark** (Activities, page 110) to make a quick, formative assessment of students' progress.
- Hide the words and ask students to write them out as you read them, encouraging them to segment each sound.
- Depending on your findings, either revisit some of the activities to reinforce any specific skill gaps, or invite students to complete an extension activity.

Extension activities

- Complete the **Spelling assessment** for further assessment of students' progress (Activities, page 116)
- Play the **Stepping stones game** (Activities, page 113).
- This game is suitable for 1–4 players and requires counters and a die.
- Students place their counters at the start of the stepping stones path. They then take turns rolling the die. They move their counter according to the number rolled.
- Upon landing on a stepping stone, the student reads the word on that stone aloud.
- If a student lands on a stone with a directional arrow, they follow the arrow forwards or backwards.
- The first student to reach the end of the stepping stones path wins.
- For those needing more support, help them to blend the letter sound or word with assistance.

PARALLEL BOOKS

In addition to Book 12a: Shep and Tosh, the following books also cover the /sh/ sound and can be used for more practice of decoding, for book bags to take home.

Dandelion Launchers
Book 12b: Fresh Fish

Dandelion Launchers Extras
Book 12a: The Shop
Book 12b: Fish Pond

Dandelion World
Book 12a: Trash in the Trench
Book 12b: Sled Dogs Dash

Dandelion Readers
Book 12: "Hush!" (Set 1 Units 11–20)
Book 12: The Cash (Set 2 Units 11–20)

LESSON PLANS

Stage 13: th

STEP 1
Preparation

20 mins

LESSON RESOURCES

Reviewing sounds (3 mins)

- Using sound cards or a whiteboard, review some previously learned words containing the /sh/ sound.

Learning goal (2 mins)

- Explain to the students that you will be teaching them to read and spell words using the consonant digraph /th/ and sounds they have previously learned.
- Introduce the book Dandelion Launchers Book 13a: This and That.
- You will be completing some activities from Dandelion Launchers Stages 8–15 Activities.

Preparation (15 mins)

- Introduce and model the new focus sound: /th/.
- 'th' can spell two different sounds: /th/ as in "that" which is voiced, and /th/ as in "thin" which is non-voiced. Ask students to listen to you say the word "that" and hear the voiced sound /th/ at the beginning of the word. Then ask them to listen to the word "thin" and hear just the air flowing at the beginning of the word.

Word building and blending

- First demonstrate how to build a word. Use only three sound cards, e.g. for the word "that."
- Draw three lines on the whiteboard, and tell the students that you are going to show them how to build the word "that."
- As you say the word slowly, move your finger under the lines.
- Ask the students to listen to the first sound in the word "that"—point to the first line. Emphasize the first sound as you say the whole word. The students respond—/th/.
- Then ask the students which letters spell the sound /th/. Remind students that two letters 't' and 'h' spell the sound /th/. Bring the letters down to the first line.
- Repeat with the second and last sounds in the word. Now ask the students to sound all three sounds and blend them into a word, moving your finger under the word: /th/ /a/ /t/ → "that."

Extension activities

1 Word reading

- Write the words you have created on the whiteboard (if you haven't done so already). Then ask students to blend and read the words.
- Show how to say each sound individually and then blend them together to read the word. Model blending by using a swishing motion with your finger.
- Encourage students to follow your example with these words: "this," "that," and "think."

2 Oral segmenting

- Say a word aloud (e.g. "this") and ask students to count the sounds in the word (3). Write the number of lines you need for all the sounds. Now ask students to listen to the sounds in the word and write a letter for every sound in the word as you spell the word.

3 Word chain

- Using sound cards or magnetic letters, demonstrate how to build the word "that." Explain to the students that you will be making one change to the word. They must be "sound detectives" and notice if you have added a sound, taken away a sound, or swapped a sound.
- Say that you are going to change the word "that" (moving your finger under the word) to "at." Ask the students to listen carefully to where the change has occurred. Move your finger under the word as you say it slowly. Once the change has been identified, invite a student to swap the sound card or letter. Ask all the students to sound out the word and read the new word, e.g. /a/ /t/ → "at."
- Direct students through the following word-chain sequence: that—at—bat—bit—bin—thin—think—thank—bank—ban—than—that

4 Reading game

- Play the game in Book 13a: This and That (pages 7–8) to familiarize students with the vocabulary in the book.

STEP 2
Application for reading
15 mins

Before reading (3 mins)

- Revisit the vocabulary taught in Step 1 (e.g. "think"). Clearly say the word: /th/ /i/ /n/ /k/
- Then provide a simple definition, e.g. "To think is to have an idea about something or someone."
- Ask questions such as What rhymes with 'think'?" and "What might you be thinking when holding an ice cream?"
- Then write the word on the whiteboard and refer back to it throughout the week for reinforcement.
- You could also draw a picture of someone thinking with a thought bubble on the whiteboard or show an actual picture.

High-frequency words (2 mins)

- Pre-teach and reiterate these high-frequency words: "to," "I," "have," "a," "of," and "the."
- Explain that these are high-frequency words that have tricky spellings the students will learn later. Read each high-frequency word aloud. Write the words on the board, showing the separate graphemes in each word.

Application (10 mins)

- The chosen text for this reading activity is Book 13a: This and That. Briefly introduce the book, its characters, and its context to spark interest and set the stage for engagement.
- Lead students through a directed reading of Book 13a: This and That. Encourage students to sound out each word carefully and then blend the sounds together to form the word.
- Provide support by modeling the blending. This hands-on practice is crucial for reinforcing phonetic skills and building fluency.
- Encourage students to sound out each word and then blend to read. This is crucial for reinforcing their learning and for building their confidence.

Extension activities

- Following the initial reading, revisit Book 13a: This and That with a focus on fluency.
- Reading the book again allows students to practice their newly acquired skills.
- Create an interactive reading environment by inviting students to take turns reading aloud. Encourage them to point to each word as they read.
- As students read more fluently, support them to read with more expression and prosody.

STEP 3
Application for spelling
15 mins

Segmenting and spelling (5 mins)

- Ask students to complete the following: **Fill in the th sound** (Activities, page 121).
- Demonstrate correct pencil grip to the class. The pencil should rest comfortably between the thumb and index finger, supported by the middle finger, with the other two fingers curled inwards. The student should have their hands resting on the table and their feet planted squarely on the floor; the paper should be at a slight angle. The student should learn to move the pencil forward using their hand muscles.
- Photocopy and distribute the **Fill in the missing sounds** activity to each student.
- Instruct students to look at each picture and use it to determine the missing sound in the corresponding word.
- Encourage the students to say the sounds as they write them and then blend the sounds in each word together as they write them.
- After students complete the activity, individually model the formation of each letter that was filled in during the activity on the whiteboard. Focus on the starting point, stroke direction, and completion of each letter.

Sentence dictation (10 mins)

- Ask students to complete **Fill in all the missing sounds** (Activities, page 122) to practice writing whole words
- Read out the **Sentence dictation** sentences (Activities, page 125): "and with nuts on the top..." and ""I think that's it. Thanks. Yum!""
- Encourage the students to sound out the words as they spell them.

Extension activities

- For students who finish early or need additional practice with letter formation, provide extra activity sheets with different words or have them create their own "missing sound" examples using words from a word bank.
- Additionally, you can create your own sentences using the learned sounds and dictate them for the students to spell.

STEP 4
Comprehension and consolidation
15 mins

Book reading (5 mins)

- Reread Book 13a: This and That.
- Revisiting the book helps to reinforce familiarity with the text and supports phonetic recognition and comprehension.

Sequencing (5 mins)

- For this activity, the students are going to retell the story, using the pictures and words in the **Retelling the story** activity (Activities, page 127).
- Divide students into small groups.
- Distribute the activity to each group.
- Decide whether to number the cards on the back to make sequencing easier for the students.
- Provide each group with a set of cards. Encourage collaboration as they work together to place the picture cards in the correct order of the story.
- Invite each group to retell the story using their arranged cards. Encourage them to use the word cards to narrate the story.
- Alternatively, after sequencing the story, the students can use the word cards to reinforce vocabulary. Ask students to match the word cards to the corresponding picture cards, promoting word recognition and comprehension.

Comprehension (5 mins)

- Check students have understood the story by completing the **Comprehension** activity (Activities, page 129).
- The aim of this activity is to reinforce vocabulary and story comprehension through a matching exercise.
- Distribute the activity to each student or small group.
- Cut out the words on the page. Then ask students to read and match them to the correct pictures.
- After matching, facilitate a discussion where students share their matches and explain their reasoning.

Extension activities

- Divide the class into pairs and give each pair a copy of the **Dice game** (Activities, page 135).
- Have students find and point to these words in Book 13a: This and That: “this,” “that,” and “think.”

STEP 5
Tracking progress

- Complete the **Bookmark** (Activities, page 134) to make a quick, formative assessment of students’ progress.
- Hide the words and ask students to write them out as you read them, encouraging them to segment each sound.
- Depending on your findings, either revisit some of the activities to reinforce any specific skill gaps, or invite students to complete an extension activity.

Extension activities

- Complete the **Spelling assessment** for further assessment of students’ progress (Activities, page 138)
- Play the **Stepping stones game** (Activities, page 133).
- This game is suitable for 1–4 players and requires counters and a die.
- Students place their counters at the start of the stepping stones path. They then take turns rolling the die. They move their counter according to the number rolled.
- Upon landing on a stepping stone, the student reads the word on that stone aloud.
- If a student lands on a stone with a directional arrow, they follow the arrow forward or backward.
- The first student to reach the end of the stepping stones path wins.
- For those needing more support, help them to blend the letter sound or word with assistance.

PARALLEL BOOKS

In addition to Book 13a: This and That, the following books also cover the /th/ sound and can be used for more practice of decoding, for book bags to take home.

Dandelion Launchers

Book 13b: Will This Fit?

Dandelion Launchers Extras

Book 13a: Thud! Crash!

Book 13b: That’s It!

Dandelion World

Book 13a: Sloths

Book 13b: The Thrill of a Run

Dandelion Readers

Book 13: The Path Up the Hill (Set 1 Units 11–20)

Book 13: Thump, Thump (Set 2 Units 11–20)

LESSON PLANS

Stage 14: ck, wh

LESSON RESOURCES

STEP 1
Preparation 20 mins

Reviewing sounds (3 mins)

- Using sound cards or a whiteboard, review some previously learned words containing the two sounds for the spelling 'th.'

Learning goal (2 mins)

- Explain to the students that you will be teaching them to read and spell words using the consonant digraphs ck and wh and sounds they have previously learned.
- Introduce the book Dandelion Launchers Book 14b: Which Shall I Pick?
- You will be completing some activities from Dandelion Launchers Stages 8–15 Activities.

Preparation (15 mins)

- Introduce the new focus spellings: 'ck' and 'wh.'
- Model how to say each sound correctly (/k/ and /w/).
- Explain that we have already learned two other ways to spell the sound /k/ (e.g. "cat" and "king").
- Explain that we have already learned another way to spell the sound /w/ as in "wind."

Word building and blending

- First demonstrate how to build a word. Use only three sound cards, e.g. for "duck."
- Draw three lines on the whiteboard, and tell the students that you are going to show them how to build the word "duck."
- As you say the word slowly, move your finger under the lines.
- Ask the students to listen to the first sound in the word "duck"—point to the first line. Emphasize the first sound as you say the whole word. The students respond—/d/.
- Then ask the students which letter spells the sound /d/. The students point to the letter (or you can tell them). Bring the letter down to the first line.
- Repeat with the second and last sounds in the word. Now ask the students to sound all three sounds and blend them into a word, moving your finger under the word:
  /d/ /u/ /ck/ → "duck"

Extension activities

1 Word reading

- Write the words you have created on the whiteboard (if you haven't done so already). Then ask students to blend and read the words.
- Show how to say each sound individually and then blend them together to read the word. Model blending by using a swishing motion with your finger.
- Encourage students to follow your example with these words: "pack," "thick," "when," and "which."

2 Oral segmenting

- Say a word aloud (e.g. "sock") and ask students to count the sounds in the word (3). Students then spell the word sound by sound. This is important as it links reading and spelling.

3 Word chain

- Using sound cards or magnetic letters, demonstrate how to build the word "lick." Explain to the students that you will be making one change to the word. They must be "sound detectives" and notice if you have added a sound, taken away a sound, or swapped a sound.
- Say that you are going to change the word "lick" (moving your finger under the word) to "click." Ask the students to listen carefully to where the change has occurred. Move your finger under the word as you say it slowly. Once the change has been identified, invite a student to swap the sound card or letter. Ask all the students to sound out the word and read the new word, e.g.
  /c/ /l/ /i/ /ck/ → "click."
- Direct students through the following word-chain sequence: lick—click—slick—slack—lack—lock—clock—clack—black—back—rack—track—trick—tick—lick

4 Reading game

- Play the game in Book 14b: Which Shall I Pick? (pages 7–8) to familiarize students with the vocabulary in the book.

STEP 2
Application for reading

15 mins

Before reading (3 mins)

- Revisit the vocabulary taught in Step 1 (e.g. "sock"). Clearly say the word: /s/ /o/ /ck/
- Then provide a simple definition, e.g. "A sock is a piece of clothing for the foot."
- Ask questions "What patterns can socks have?" and "What else do you wear on your feet?"
- Then write the word on the whiteboard and refer back to it throughout the week for reinforcement.
- You could also draw a picture of someone thinking with a sock on the whiteboard or show an actual picture.

High-frequency words (2 mins)

- Pre-teach and reiterate these high-frequency words: "cold," "he," "to," "the," "I," and "put."
- Explain that these are high-frequency words that have tricky spellings the students will learn later. Read each high-frequency word aloud. Write the words on the board, showing the separate graphemes in each word.

Application (10 mins)

- The chosen text for this reading activity is Book 14b: Which Shall I Pick? Briefly introduce the book, its characters, and its context to spark interest and set the stage for engagement.
- Lead students through a directed reading of Book 14b: Which Shall I Pick? Encourage students to sound out each word carefully and then blend the sounds together to form the word.
- Provide support by modeling the blending. This hands-on practice is crucial for reinforcing phonetic skills and building fluency.
- Encourage students to sound out each word and then blend to read. This is crucial for reinforcing their learning and for building their confidence.

Extension activities

- Following the initial reading, revisit Book 14b: Which Shall I Pick? with a focus on fluency.
- Reading the book again allows students to practice their newly acquired skills.
- Create an interactive reading environment by inviting students to take turns reading aloud. Encourage them to point to each word as they read.
- As students read more fluently, support them to read with more expression and prosody.

STEP 3
Application for spelling

15 mins

Segmenting and spelling (5 mins)

- Ask students to complete the following: **Fill in the ck sound** (Activities, page 145).
- Demonstrate correct pencil grip to the class. The pencil should rest comfortably between the thumb and index finger, supported by the middle finger, with the other two fingers curled inwards. The student should have their hands resting on the table and their feet planted squarely on the floor; the paper should be at a slight angle. The student should learn to move the pencil forward using their hand muscles.
- Distribute the **Fill in the missing sounds** activity to each student.
- Instruct students to look at each picture and use it to determine the missing sound in the corresponding word.
- Encourage the students to say the sounds as they write them and then blend the sounds in each word together as they write them.
- After students complete the activity, individually model the formation of each letter that was filled in during the activity on the whiteboard. Focus on the starting point, stroke direction, and completion of each letter.

Sentence dictation (10 mins)

- Ask students to complete **Fill in all the missing sounds** (Activities, page 146) to practice writing whole words
- Read out the **Sentence dictation** sentences (Activities, page 151): "'Jim put on the thick socks and the black socks." and "When Jim left the sock shop, he had lots of socks!"
- Encourage the students to sound out the words as they spell them.

Extension activities

- For students who finish early or need additional practice with letter formation, provide extra activity sheets with different words or have them create their own "missing sound" examples using words from a word bank.
- Additionally, you can create your own sentences using the learned sounds and dictate them for the students to spell.

STEP 4
Comprehension and consolidation

15 mins

Book reading (5 mins)

- Reread Book 14b: Which Shall I Pick?
- Revisiting the book helps to reinforce familiarity with the text and supports phonetic recognition and comprehension.

Sequencing (5 mins)

- For this activity, the students are going to retell the story, using the pictures and words in the **Retelling the story** activity (Activities, page 153).
- Divide students into small groups.
- Distribute the activity to each group.
- Decide whether to number the cards on the back to make sequencing easier for the students.
- Provide each group with a set of cards. Encourage collaboration as they work together to place the picture cards in the correct order of the story.
- Invite each group to retell the story using their arranged cards. Encourage them to use the word cards to narrate the story.
- Alternatively, after sequencing the story, the students can use the word cards to reinforce vocabulary. Ask students to match the word cards to the corresponding picture cards, promoting word recognition and comprehension.

Comprehension (5 mins)

- Check students have understood the story by completing the **Comprehension** activity (Activities, page 155).
- The aim of this activity is to reinforce vocabulary and story comprehension through a matching exercise.
- Distribute the activity to each student or small group.
- Cut out the words on the page. Then ask students to read and match them to the correct pictures.
- After matching, facilitate a discussion where students share their matches and explain their reasoning.

Extension activities

- Divide the class into pairs and give each pair a copy of the **Dice game** (Activities, page 161).
- Have students find and point to these words in Book 14b: Which Shall I Pick? "socks," "pack," and "thick."

STEP 5
Tracking progress

- Complete the **Bookmark** (Activities, page 160) to make a quick, formative assessment of students' progress.
- Hide the words and ask students to write them out as you read them, encouraging them to segment each sound.
- Depending on your findings, either revisit some of the activities to reinforce any specific skill gaps, or invite students to complete an extension activity.

Extension activities

- Complete the **Spelling assessment** for further assessment of students' progress (Activities, page 164)
- Play the **Stepping stones game** (Activities, page 158).
- This game is suitable for 1–4 players and requires counters and a die.
- Students place their counters at the start of the stepping stones path. They then take turns rolling the die. They move their counter according to the number rolled.
- Upon landing on a stepping stone, the student reads the word on that stone aloud.
- If a student lands on a stone with a directional arrow, they follow the arrow forwards or backwards.
- The first student to reach the end of the stepping stones path wins.
- For those needing more support, help them to blend the letter sound or word with assistance.

PARALLEL BOOKS

In addition to Book 14b: Which Shall I Pick?, the following books also cover the 'ck' or 'wh' spellings and can be used for more practice of decoding, for book bags to take home.

Dandelion Launchers

Book 14a: The Back Pack

Dandelion Launchers Extras

Book 14a: The Clock

Book 14b: When Can I Get On?

Dandelion World

Book 14a: Shells and Rocks

Book 14b: Flick the Puck

Dandelion Readers

Book 14: The Trick (Set 1 Units 11–20)

Book 14: Raj Gets a Shock (Set 2 Units 11–20)

Stage 15: ng, qu

STEP 1
Preparation

20 mins

Reviewing sounds (3 mins)

- Using sound cards or a whiteboard, review some previously learned words containing the 'ck' and 'wh' spellings.

Learning goal (2 mins)

- Explain to the students that you will be teaching them to read and spell words using the consonant digraphs ng and qu and sounds they have previously learned.
- Introduce the book Dandelion Launchers Book 15b: The Strong Wind.
- You will be completing some activities from Dandelion Launchers Stages 8–15 Activities.

Preparation (15 mins)

- Introduce and model the new focus sounds: /ng/ and /qu/. Note: the letters 'qu' spell two sounds (/k/ and /w/), but we teach them together because they usually appear together in words.

Word building and blending

- First demonstrate how to build a word. Use only three sound cards, e.g. for the word "quip."
- Draw three lines on the whiteboard, and tell the students that you are going to show them how to build the word "quip."
- As you say the word slowly, move your finger under the lines.
- Ask the students to listen to the first sound in the word "quip"—point to the first line. Emphasize the first sound as you say the whole word. The students respond—/qu/.
- Then ask the students which letters spell this sound. The students point to the letters (or you can tell them). Bring the letters down to the first line.
- Repeat with the second and last sounds in the word. Now ask the students to sound all three sounds and blend them into a word, moving your finger under the word: /qu/ /i/ /p/ → "quip"
- The next time this is done, you can ask a student to participate and identify the sound and then letter and bring it down to the line.

Extension activities

1 Word reading

- Write the words you have created on the whiteboard (if you haven't done so already). Then ask students to blend and read the words.
- Show how to say each sound individually and then blend them together to read the word. Model blending by using a swishing motion with your finger.
- Encourage students to follow your example with these words: "ding," "rings," "quit," and "quick."

2 Oral segmenting

- Say a word aloud (e.g. "quilt") and ask students to count to sounds in the word (4). Write the number of lines you need for all the sounds. Now ask students to listen to the sounds in the word and write a letter for every sound in the word as you spell the word.
- You may need to explain that /qu/ is two sounds: /k/ and /w/.

3 Word chain

- Using sound cards or magnetic letters, demonstrate how to build the word "sing." Explain to the students that you will be making one change to the word. They must be "sound detectives" and notice if you have added a sound, taken away a sound, or swapped a sound.
- Say that you are going to change the word "sing" (moving your finger under the word) to "sling." Ask the students to listen carefully to where the change has occurred. Move your finger under the word as you say it slowly. Once the change has been identified, invite a student to swap the letter card or letter. Ask all the students to sound out the word and read the new word, e.g. /s/ /l/ /i/ /ng/ → "sing."
- Direct students through the following word-chain sequence: sing—sling—slang—sang—song—pong—ping—wing—swing—sing

4 Reading game

- Play the game in Book 15b: The Strong Wind (pages 7–8) to familiarize students with the vocabulary in the book.

LESSON RESOURCES

STEP 2
Application for reading
15 mins

Before reading (3 mins)

- Revisit the vocabulary taught in Step 1 (e.g. "sing"). Clearly say the word: /s/ /i/ /ng/
- Then provide a simple definition, e.g. "To sing is to make a musical sound with your voice."
- Ask questions "What is your favorite song?" and "When might you sing on someone's birthday?"
- Then write the word on the whiteboard and refer back to it throughout the week for reinforcement.
- You could also draw a picture of someone singing into a microphone on the whiteboard or show an actual picture.

High-frequency words (2 mins)

- Pre-teach and reiterate these high-frequency words: "I," "have," "you," "do," "to," "was," "he," "said," "the," "a," "she," "cannot," and "yelled."
- Explain that these are high-frequency words that have tricky spellings the students will learn later. Read each high-frequency word aloud. Write the words on the board, showing the separate graphemes in each word.

Application (10 mins)

- The chosen text for this reading activity is Book 15b: The Strong Wind. Briefly introduce the book, its characters, and its context to spark interest and set the stage for engagement.
- Lead students through a directed reading of Book 15b: The Strong Wind. Encourage students to sound out each word carefully and then blend the sounds together to form the word.
- Provide support by modeling the blending. This hands-on practice is crucial for reinforcing phonetic skills and building fluency.
- Encourage students to sound out each word and then blend to read. This is crucial for reinforcing their learning and for building their confidence.

Extension activities

- Following the initial reading, revisit Book 15b: The Strong Wind with a focus on fluency.
- Reading the book again allows students to practice their newly acquired skills.
- Create an interactive reading environment by inviting students to take turns reading aloud. Encourage them to point to each word as they read.
- As students read more fluently, support them to read with more expression and prosody.

STEP 3
Application for spelling
15 mins

Segmenting and spelling (5 mins)

- Ask students to complete the following: **Fill in the ng sound** (Activities, page 169).
- Demonstrate correct pencil grip to the class. The pencil should rest comfortably between the thumb and index finger, supported by the middle finger, with the other two fingers curled inwards. The student should have their hands resting on the table and their feet planted squarely on the floor; the paper should be at a slight angle. The student should learn to move the pencil forward using their hand muscles.
- Distribute the **Fill in the missing sounds** activity to each student.
- Instruct students to look at each picture and use it to determine the missing sound in the corresponding word.
- Encourage the students to say the sounds as they write them and then blend the sounds in each word together as they write them.
- After students complete the activity, individually model the formation of each letter that was filled in during the activity on the whiteboard. Focus on the starting point, stroke direction, and completion of each letter.

Sentence dictation (10 mins)

- Ask students to complete **Fill in all the missing sounds** (Activities, page 170) to practice writing whole words
- Read out the **Sentence dictation** sentences (Activities, page 174): "Dot rang up a long stem. Dot did not quit the song." and "Then Dot felt a strong wind. She hung from the stem."
- Encourage the students to sound out the words as they spell them.

Extension activities

- For students who finish early or need additional practice with letter formation, provide extra activity sheets with different words or have them create their own "missing sound" examples using words from a word bank.
- Additionally, you can create your own sentences using the learned sounds and dictate them for the students to spell.

STEP 4
Comprehension and consolidation

15 mins

Book reading (5 mins)

- Reread Book 15b: The Strong Wind.
- Revisiting the book helps to reinforce familiarity with the text and supports phonetic recognition and comprehension.

Sequencing (5 mins)

- For this activity, the students are going to retell the story, using the pictures and words in the **Retelling the story** activity (Activities, page 176).
- Divide students into small groups.
- Distribute the activity to each group.
- Decide whether to number the cards on the back to make sequencing easier for the students.
- Provide each group with a set of cards. Encourage collaboration as they work together to place the picture cards in the correct order of the story.
- Invite each group to retell the story using their arranged cards. Encourage them to use the word cards to narrate the story.
- Alternatively, after sequencing the story, the students can use the word cards to reinforce vocabulary. Ask students to match the word cards to the corresponding picture cards, promoting word recognition and comprehension.

Comprehension (5 mins)

- Check students have understood the story by completing the **Comprehension** activity (Activities, page 178).
- The aim of this activity is to reinforce vocabulary and story comprehension through a matching exercise.
- Distribute the activity to each student or small group.
- Cut out the words on the page. Then ask students to read and match them to the correct pictures.
- After matching, facilitate a discussion where students share their matches and explain their reasoning.

Extension activities

- Divide the class into pairs and give each pair a copy of the **Dice game** (Activities, page 183).
- Have students find and point to these words in Book 15b: The Strong Wind: "song," "sang," "hung," "quit," and "quick."

STEP 5
Tracking progress

- Complete the **Bookmark** (Activities, page 182) to make a quick, formative assessment of students' progress.
- Hide the words and ask students to write them out as you read them, encouraging them to segment each sound.
- For a summative assessment of each student's progress, assign the Stages 11–15 Assessment (page 77).
- Then for a summative assessment of Stages 1–7, assign the **Reading Assessment** on page 59.

Extension activities

- Complete the **Spelling assessment** for further assessment of students' progress (Activities, page 186)
- Play the **Stepping stones game** (Activities, page 181).
- This game is suitable for 1–4 players and requires counters and a die.
- Students place their counters at the start of the stepping stones path. They then take turns rolling the die. They move their counter according to the number rolled.
- Upon landing on a stepping stone, the student reads the word on that stone aloud.
- If a student lands on a stone with a directional arrow, they follow the arrow forwards or backwards.
- The first student to reach the end of the stepping stones path wins.

PARALLEL BOOKS

In addition to Book 15b: The Strong Wind, the following books also cover the /ng/ or /qu/ sounds and can be used for more practice of decoding, for book bags to take home.

Dandelion Launchers
Book 15a: Ding Dong

Dandelion Launchers Extras
Book 15a: Spring
Book 15b: Ting-a-ling

Dandelion World
Book 15a: Spring Has Sprung
Book 15b: Long Bat Wings

Dandelion Readers
Book 15: The Ring (Set 1 Units 11–20)
Book 16: The Quest (Set 2 Units 11–20)
Book 15: The Sting (Set 1 Units 11–20)
Book 16: The Quilt (Set 2 Units 11–20)

a–e

STEP 1
Preparation 20 mins

Learning goal (2 mins)

- Explain to the students that you will be teaching them to read and spell new words using the spelling 'a–e' for the sound /ae/.
- Introduce the book Dandelion Readers VCe Spellings Book 1: Late.
- You will be completing some activities from Dandelion Readers VCe Spellings Activities.

Preparation (18 mins)

- Introduce the spelling 'a–e' for the sound /ae/.
- Model the sound correctly and ask students to copy.
- For example, say, "This letter stands for the sound /ae/ as in 'late.' Watch my mouth as I say the sound."
- Read this list of words: "late," "cake," and "plate." For each, point to the letters as you slowly pronounce them, demonstrating how the 'a' and 'e' work together to form the /ae/ sound. Use your thumb and third finger to visually link these letters.

Word building and blending

- Assign the **Word-building and blending** activity (Activities, page 6).
- Ask the students to cut out the letters along the dotted lines, which split the 'a' and 'e.'
- For example, demonstrate with the word "gate" how to separate 'a' from 'e' and then rearrange them by placing 'e' at the end after the 't.' Use your fingers to reinforce the connection between letters. Draw a link between the 'a' and the 'e' to remind students that 'a-e' is one spelling that has been split.

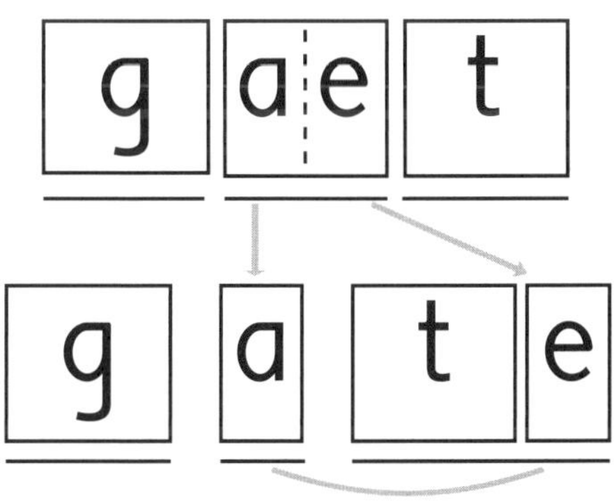

- For the remaining words, direct students through the process of assembling the cut-out letters, always emphasizing how the 'a' and 'e' are connected.

LESSON RESOURCES

- Explain the spelling rule: even though the letter 't' separates the vowels, the 'a' and 'e' still work together to form the /ae/ sound.

Extension activities

1 Word reading

- Write the words you have created on the whiteboard. Then ask students to blend and read the words.
- Show how to say each sound individually and then blend them together to read the word. Model blending by using a swishing motion with your finger.
- Encourage students to follow your example with these words: "name" and "tale."

2 Oral segmenting

- Say a word aloud (e.g. "cake") and count the sounds in the word (3). Write the number of lines you need for all the sounds. Now ask students to listen to the sounds in the word and write a letter for every sound in the word as you spell the word.

3 Word chain

- Using sound cards or magnetic letters, demonstrate how to build the word "gate." Explain to the students that you will be making one change to the word. They must be "sound detectives" and notice if you have added a sound, taken away a sound, or swapped a sound.
- Say that you are going to change the word "gate" (moving your finger under the word) to "grate." Ask the students to listen carefully to where the change has occurred. Move your finger under the word as you say it slowly. Once the change has been identified, invite a student to swap the sound card or letter. Ask all the students to sound out the word and read the new word, e.g. /g/ /r/ /ae/ /t/ → "grate."
- Direct students through the following word-chain sequence: gate—grate—rate—ate—mate—mane—bane—pane—plane—lane—late—gate

STEP 2
Application for reading
15 mins

Before reading (3 mins)

- Revisit the vocabulary taught in Step 1 (e.g. "wake"). Clearly say the word: /w/ /ae/ /k/. Then explore different meanings for the word "wake," such as waking from sleep, or a trail of disturbed water created by a boat.
- Ask questions such as, "When do you wake up?"
- Then write the word on the whiteboard and refer back to it throughout the week for reinforcement.

High-frequency words (2 mins)

- Pre-teach or reiterate these high-frequency words: "a," "was," "he," "for," "school," "birthday," "no," "said," "the," "his," "they," "she," "goal," and "day."
- Explain that these are high-frequency words that have tricky spellings the students will learn later. Read each high-frequency word aloud.
- Write the words on the board, showing the separate graphemes in each word. As students learn more of the Alphabetic Code, they will be able to decode those graphemes.

Application (10 mins)

- Once students have started to learn and blend words using the sounds learned in this lesson plan, it's important to provide them with opportunities for them to use their newly acquired skills.
- The chosen text for this reading activity is Book 1: Late. Briefly introduce the book, its characters, and its context to spark interest and set the stage for engagement.
- Lead students through a directed reading of Book 1: Late. Encourage students to sound out each word carefully and then blend the sounds together to form the word.
- Provide support by modeling the blending. This hands-on practice is crucial for reinforcing phonetic skills and building fluency.
- Encourage students to sound out each word and then blend to read. This is crucial for reinforcing their learning and for building their confidence.

Extension activities

- Complete the **Fluency** activity (Activities, page 18) to develop students' fluency and prosody skills.
- Create an interactive reading environment by inviting students to take turns reading aloud.

STEP 3
Application for spelling
15 mins

Segmenting and spelling (5 mins)

- Ask students to complete the following activity to practice writing whole words: **Segmenting and spelling** (Activities, page 7).
- In the activity each word is associated with a picture as a visual clue.
- Task students with filling in the squares with the appropriate spelling for each sound.
- Demonstrate correct pencil grip to the class. The pencil should rest comfortably between the thumb and index finger, supported by the middle finger, with the other two fingers curled inwards. The student should have their hands resting on the table and their feet planted squarely on the floor; the paper should be at a slight angle. The student should learn to move the pencil forward using their hand muscles.
- Encourage the students to say the sounds as they write them and then blend the sounds in each word together as they write them.
- After students complete the activity, individually model the formation of each letter that was filled in during the activity on the whiteboard. Focus on the starting point, stroke direction, and completion of each letter.

Sentence dictation (10 mins)

- Read out the **Sentence dictation** sentences (Activities, page 19): "The box had a clock in it! Frank was not late for the next game."
- Encourage the students to sound out the words as they spell them.
- Repeat the sentence if necessary, or read it out in phrases to allow students who may need additional time to process the information.
- For students who finish early or need additional practice with letter formation, you can create your own sentences using the learned sounds and dictate them for the students to spell.

Extension activities

- Ask students to complete the **Punctuation** activity (Activities, page 20).
- Remind students that capital letters are used at the beginning of sentences, and periods are used at the end of sentences.
- Encourage the students to read the passage aloud, as this will help them to identify where the sentences stop.

STEP 4
Comprehension and consolidation
15 mins

Book reading (5 mins)

- Reread Book 1: Late.
- Revisiting the book helps to reinforce familiarity with the text and supports phonetic recognition and comprehension.
- For students who need assistance, pair them with a poor or an adult to support their reading.

Comprehension (5 mins)

- Ask students to complete **Make a page for a comic** (Activities, page 16).
- Distribute the activity to each student.
- Explain that the comic provided has illustrations missing.
- Ask the students to read the text and draw a picture to match the text in each box.

Extension activities

1 Find the untruths

- Check students have understood the story by instructing them to complete **Find the untruths** (Activities, page 17).
- In this activity, the students are provided with a passage with four untruths in it.
- Ask the students to read the text carefully and underline the falsehoods planted in the story.

2 4-in-a-row game

- Divide the class into pairs and give each pair a copy of the **4-in-a-row game** (Activities, page 22).
- Play with two sets of colored counters. The two players take turns to read the word and put a counter on the word.
- Players can make 4-in-a-row horizontally, vertically and diagonally. The winner is the first to get four of their counters in a row.
- The winner places a counter on a ball. The game is played until all the balls are covered.

3 Write the story

- Invite students to complete the **Write the story in your own words** activity (Activites, page 21).
- Distribute the activity to each student.
- Encourage students to first retell the story orally before writing it down.

STEP 5
Tracking progress

- Assign the **Timed word reading** (Activities, page 12). Students can repeat this activity to improve their reading speed.
- To ensure students are confident with the new sounds, blending, and segmenting, complete the **Spelling assessment and bookmarks** (Activities, page 24) to make a quick, formative assessment of their progress.
- Ask students to read and then blend each of the words.
- Hide the words and ask students to write them out as you read them, encouraging them to segment each sound.
- Depending on your findings, either revisit some of the activities to reinforce any specific skill gaps, or invite students to complete an additional activity from the Activities book.

Extension activities

1 Stepping stones game

- Play the **Stepping stones game** (Activities, page 22).
- This game is suitable for 1–4 players and requires counters and a die.
- Students place their counters at the start of the stepping stones path. They then take turns rolling the die. They move their counter according to the number rolled.
- Upon landing on a stepping stone, the student reads the word on that stone aloud.
- If a student lands on a stone with a directional arrow, they follow the arrow forward or backward.
- The first student to reach the end of the stepping stones path wins.
- Provide positive feedback and encouragement throughout the game.
- For those needing more support, help them to blend the letter sound or word with assistance.

2 Certificates and progress tracking

- Print the **Reading certificate** (Activities, page 130) for students to take home.
- Ask students to check Book 1 on their **Bookmark** (Activities, page 128)
- Check Book 1 on the **Check sheet** (Activities, page 129).

LESSON PLANS

e–e

STEP 1
Preparation

20 mins

LESSON RESOURCES

Learning goal (2 mins)

- Explain to the students that you will be teaching them to read and spell new words using the spelling ‘e–e’ for the sound /ee/.
- Introduce the book Dandelion Readers VCe Spellings Book 2: Pete.
- You will be completing some activities from Dandelion Readers VCe Spellings Activities.

Preparation (18 mins)

- Introduce the spelling ‘e–e’ for the sound /ee/.
- Model the sound correctly and ask students to copy.
- For example, say, “This letter stands for the sound /ee/ as in ‘Pete.’ Watch my mouth as I say the sound.”
- Read this list of names: “Pete,” “Eve,” and “Steve.” For each, point to the letters as you slowly pronounce them, demonstrating how the two ‘e’ letters work together to form the /ee/ sound. Use your thumb and third finger to visually link these letters.

Word building and blending

- Assign the **Word-building and blending** activity (Activities, page 6).
- Ask the students to cut out the letters along the dotted lines, which split the ‘e’ and ‘e.’
- For example, demonstrate with the word “Pete” how to separate two ‘e’ letters’ and then rearrange them by placing ‘e’ at the end after the ‘t.’ Use your fingers to reinforce the connection between letters. Draw a link between the two ‘e’ letters to remind students that ‘e-e’ is one spelling that has been split.

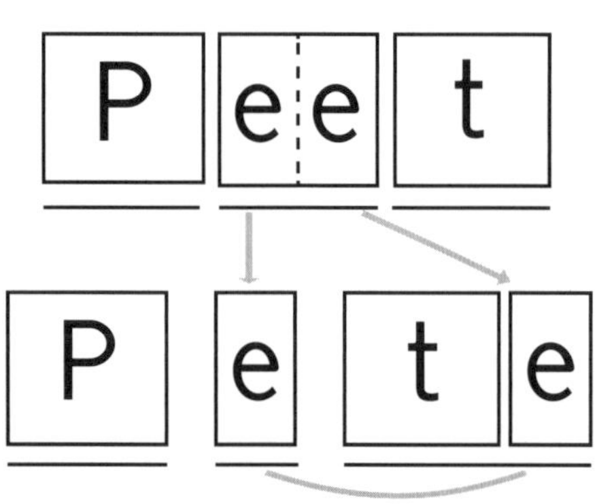

- For the remaining words, direct students through the process of assembling the cut-out letters, always emphasizing how the two ‘e’ letters are connected.
- Explain the spelling rule: even though the letter ‘t’ separates the vowels, the two ‘e’ letters still together form the /ee/ sound.

Extension activities

1 Word reading

- Write the words you have created on the whiteboard (if you haven’t done so already). Then ask students to blend and read the words.
- Show how to say each sound individually and then blend them together to read the word. Model blending by using a swishing motion with your finger.
- Encourage students to follow your example with these words: “Pete,” “Eve,” and “theme.”

2 Oral segmenting

- Say a word aloud (e.g. “delete”) count the sounds in the word (5). Write the number of lines you need for all the sounds. Now ask students to listen to the sounds in the word and write a letter for every sound in the word as you spell the word.

3 Word chain

- Using sound cards or magnetic letters, demonstrate how to build the word “these.” Explain to the students that you will be making one change to the word. They must be “sound detectives” and notice if you have added a sound, taken away a sound, or swapped a sound.
- Say that you are going to change the word “these” (moving your finger under the word) to “theme.” Ask the students to listen carefully to where the change has occurred. Move your finger under the words as you say it slowly. Once the change has been identified, invite a student to swap the sound card or letter. Ask all the students to sound out the word and read the new word, e.g. /th/ /ee/ /m/ → “theme.”
- Direct students through the following word-chain sequence: these—theme—meme—deme—theme—these

STEP 2
Application for reading

15 mins

Before reading (3 mins)

- Revisit the vocabulary taught in Step 1 (e.g. "delete"). Clearly say the word: /d/ /e/ /l/ /ee/ /t/. Then provide a simple definition: "To delete something is to remove it."
- Ask questions such as, "When have you deleted something?"
- Then write the word on the whiteboard and refer back to it throughout the week for reinforcement.

High-frequency words (2 mins)

- Pre-teach or reiterate these high-frequency words: "is," "I'll," "make," "to," "said," "his," "he," "the," "began," "boots," "no," and "do."
- Explain that these are high-frequency words that have tricky spellings the students will learn later. Read each high-frequency word aloud.
- Write the words on the board, showing the separate graphemes in each word. As students learn more of the Alphabetic Code, they will be able to decode those graphemes.

Application (10 mins)

- Once students have started to learn and blend words using the sounds learned in this lesson plan, it's important to provide them with opportunities for them to use their newly acquired skills.
- The chosen text for this reading activity is Book 2: Pete. Briefly introduce the book, its characters, and its context to spark interest and set the stage for engagement.
- Lead students through a directed reading of Book 2: Pete. Encourage students to sound out each word carefully and then blend the sounds together to form the word.
- Provide support by modeling the blending. This hands-on practice is crucial for reinforcing phonetic skills and building fluency.
- Encourage students to sound out each word and then blend to read. This is crucial for reinforcing their learning and for building their confidence.

Extension activities

- Complete the **Fluency** activity (Activities, page 38) to develop students' fluency and prosody skills.
- Create an interactive reading environment by inviting students to take turns reading aloud.

STEP 3
Application for spelling

15 mins

Reading and sorting (5 mins)

- Ask students to complete the following activity: **Reading and sorting** (Activities, page 10).
- In the activity, the students are provided with a list of words with 'e' spellings and 'e–e' spellings, which they have to sort according to their different sounds: /e/ and /ee/, respectively.
- Distribute the activity to each student or small group.
- Cut the words into reading cards.
- Read the words aloud and ask the students to sort the words according to whether they hear an /e/ sound or an /ee/ sounds.
- Emphasize that the e–e spelling makes the /ee/ sound.

Sentence dictation (10 mins)

- Read out the **Sentence dictation** sentences (Activities, page 39): "Pete began to help, but the dishes cracked. Dad had to press 'delete' to stop him!"
- Encourage the students to sound out the words as they spell them.
- Demonstrate correct pencil grip to the class. The pencil should rest comfortably between the thumb and index finger, supported by the middle finger, with the other two fingers curled inwards. The student should have their hands resting on the table and their feet planted squarely on the floor; the paper should be at a slight angle. The student should learn to move the pencil forward using their hand muscles.
- Encourage the students to say the sounds as they write them and then blend the three sounds in each word together as they write them.
- After students complete the activity, individually model the formation of each letter that was filled in during the activity on the whiteboard. Focus on the starting point, stroke direction, and completion of each letter.

Extension activities

- For students who finish early or need additional practice with letter formation, you can create your own sentences using the learned sounds and dictate them for the students to spell.

STEP 4
Comprehension and consolidation
15 mins

Book reading (5 mins)

- Reread Book 2: Pete.
- Revisiting the book helps to reinforce familiarity with the text and supports phonetic recognition and comprehension.
- For students who need assistance, pair them with a peer or an adult to support their reading.

Comprehension (5 mins)

- Ask students to complete **Make a page for a comic** (Activities, page 35).
- Distribute the activity to each student.
- Explain that the comic provided has illustrations missing.
- Ask the students to read the text and draw a picture to match the text in each box.

Extension activities

1 Find the untruths

- Check students have understood the story by instructing them to complete **Find the untruths** (Activities, page 37).
- In this activity, the students are provided with a passage with four untruths in it.
- Ask the students to read the text carefully and underline the falsehoods planted in the story.

2 4-in-a-row game

- Divide the class into pairs and give each pair a copy of the **4-in-a-row game** (Activities, page 43).
- Play with two sets of colored counters. The two players take turns to read the word and put a counter on the word.
- Players can make 4-in-a-row horizontally, vertically and diagonally. The winner is the first to get four of their counters in a row.
- The winner places a counter on a ball. The game is played until all the balls are covered.

3 Write the story

- Invite students to complete the **Write the story in your own words** activity (Activites, page 41).
- Distribute the activity to each student.
- Encourage students to first retell the story orally before writing it down.

STEP 5
Tracking progress

- Assign the **Timed word reading** (Activities, page 32). Students can repeat this activity to improve their reading speed.
- To ensure students are confident with the new sounds, blending, and segmenting, complete the **Spelling assessment and bookmarks** (Activities, page 44) to make a quick, formative assessment of their progress.
- Ask students to read and then blend each of the words.
- Hide the words and ask students to write them out as you read them, encouraging them to segment each sound.
- Depending on your findings, either revisit some of the activities to reinforce any specific skill gaps, or invite students to complete an additional activity from the Activities book.

Extension activities

1 Stepping stones game

- Play the **Stepping stones game** (Activities, page 42).
- This game is suitable for 1–4 players and requires counters and a die.
- Students place their counters at the start of the stepping stones path. They then take turns rolling the die. They move their counter according to the number rolled.
- Upon landing on a stepping stone, the student reads the word on that stone aloud.
- If a student lands on a stone with a directional arrow, they follow the arrow forward or backward.
- The first student to reach the end of the stepping stones path wins.
- Provide positive feedback and encouragement throughout the game.
- For those needing more support, help them to blend the letter sound or word with assistance.

2 Certificates and progress tracking

- Print the **Reading certificate** (Activities, page 131) for students to take home.
- Ask students to check Book 2 on their **Bookmark** (Activities, page 128)
- Check Book 2 on the **Check sheet** (Activities, page 129).

i–e

STEP 1
Preparation

20 mins

LESSON RESOURCES

Learning goal (2 mins)

- Explain to the students that you will be teaching them to read and spell new words using the spelling 'i–e' for the sound /ie/.
- Introduce the book Dandelion Readers VCe Spellings Book 3: A Fine Life.
- You will be completing some activities from Dandelion Readers VCe Spellings Activities.

Preparation (18 mins)

- Introduce the spelling 'i–e' for the sound /ie/.
- Model the sound correctly and ask students to copy.
- For example, say, "This letter stands for the sound /ie/ as in 'life.' Watch my mouth as I say the sound."
- Read this list of words: "life," "time," and "shine." For each, point to the letters as you slowly pronounce them, demonstrating how the 'i' and 'e' work together to form the /ie/ sound. Use your thumb and third finger to visually link these letters.

Word building and blending

- Assign the **Word-building and blending** activity (Activities, page 46).
- Ask the students to cut out the letters along the dotted lines, which split the 'i' and 'e.'
- For example, demonstrate with the word "dive" how to separate 'i' from 'e' and then rearrange them by placing 'e' at the end after the 'v.' Use your fingers to reinforce the connection between letters. Draw a link between the 'i' and the 'e' to remind students that 'i-e' is one spelling that has been split.

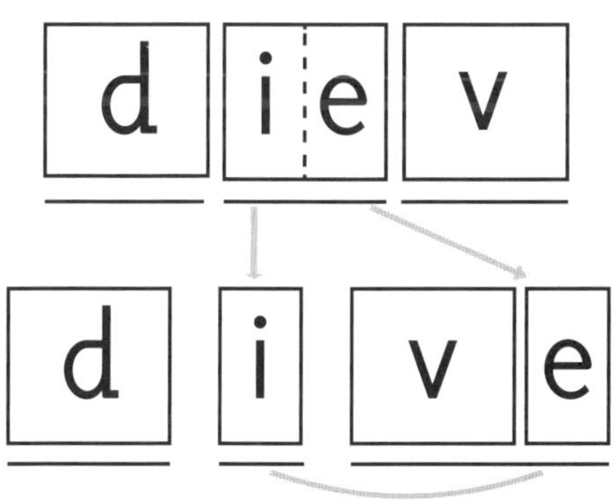

- For the remaining words, direct students through the process of assembling the cut-out letters, always emphasizing how the 'i' and 'e' are connected.
- Explain the spelling rule: even though the letter 'v' separates the vowels, the 'i' and 'e' still work together to form the /ie/ sound.

Extension activities

1 Word reading

- Write the words you have created on the whiteboard. Then ask students to blend and read the words.
- Show how to say each sound individually and then blend them together to read the word. Model blending by using a swishing motion with your finger.
- Encourage students to follow your example with these words: "wife" and "glide."

2 Oral segmenting

- Say a word aloud (e.g. "kite") and count the sounds in the word (3). Write the number of lines you need for all the sounds. Now ask students to listen to the sounds in the word and write a letter for every sound in the word as you spell the word.

3. Word chain

- Using sound cards or magnetic letters, demonstrate how to build the word "spine." Explain to the students that you will be making one change to the word. They must be "sound detectives" and notice if you have added a sound, taken away a sound, or swapped a sound.
- Say that you are going to change the word "spine" (moving your finger under the word) to "pine." Ask the students to listen carefully to where the change has occurred. Move your finger under the word as you say it slowly. Once the change has been identified, invite a student to swap the sound card or letter. Ask all the students to sound out the word and read the new word, e.g. /p/ /ie/ /n/ → "pine."
- Direct students through the following word-chain sequence of words: spine—pine—fine—mine—mite—site—spite—spine

STEP 2
Application for reading

15 mins

Before reading (3 mins)

- Revisit the vocabulary taught in Step 1 (e.g. "pipe"). Clearly say the word: /p/ /ie/ /p/. Explore different definitions for pipe, such as a musical instrument or a tube used for carrying substances.
- Ask questions such as, "What are pipes used for?"
- Then write the word on the whiteboard and refer back to it throughout the week for reinforcement.

High-frequency words (2 mins)

- Pre-teach or reiterate these high-frequency words: "his," "were," "little," "they," "lived," "of," "leaves," "he," "to," "the," "we," "my," "said," "politely," "be," and "baby.
- Explain that these are high-frequency words that have tricky spellings the students will learn later. Read each high-frequency word aloud.
- Write the words on the board, showing the separate graphemes in each word. As students learn more of the Alphabetic Code, they will be able to decode those graphemes.

Application (10 mins)

- Once students have started to learn and blend words using the sounds learned in this lesson plan, it's important to provide them with opportunities for them to use their newly acquired skills.
- The chosen text for this reading activity is Book 3: A Fine Life. Briefly introduce the book, its characters, and its context to spark interest and set the stage for engagement.
- Lead students through a directed reading of Book 3: A Fine Life. Encourage students to sound out each word carefully and then blend the sounds together to form the word.
- Provide support by modeling the blending. This hands-on practice is crucial for reinforcing phonetic skills and building fluency.
- Encourage students to sound out each word and then blend to read. This is crucial for reinforcing their learning and for building their confidence.

Extension activities

- Complete the **Fluency** activity (Activities, page 58) to develop students' fluency and prosody skills.
- Create an interactive reading environment by inviting students to take turns reading aloud.

STEP 3
Application for spelling

15 mins

Segmenting and spelling (5 mins)

- Ask students to complete the following activity to practice writing whole words: **Segmenting and spelling** (Activities, page 47).
- In the activity each word is associated with a picture as a visual clue.
- Task students with filling in the squares with the appropriate spelling for each sound.
- Demonstrate correct pencil grip to the class. The pencil should rest comfortably between the thumb and index finger, supported by the middle finger, with the other two fingers curled inwards. The student should have their hands resting on the table and their feet planted squarely on the floor; the paper should be at a slight angle. The student should learn to move the pencil forward using their hand muscles.
- Encourage the students to say the sounds as they write them and then blend the sounds in each word together as they write them.
- After students complete the activity, individually model the formation of each letter that was filled in during the activity on the whiteboard. Focus on the starting point, stroke direction, and completion of each letter.

Sentence dictation (10 mins)

- Read out the **Sentence dictation** sentences (Activities, page 59): "Mike and his wife, Sunshine, were fine little mice. They lived in a nest in a pile of leaves."
- Encourage the students to sound out the words as they spell them.
- Repeat the sentence if necessary, or read it out in phrases to allow students who may need additional time to process the information.
- For students who finish early or need additional practice with letter formation, you can create your own sentences using the learned sounds and dictate them for the students to spell.

Extension activities

- Ask students to complete the **Punctuation** activity (Activities, page 60).
- Remind students that capital letters are used at the beginning of sentences, and periods are used at the end of sentences.
- Encourage the students to read the passage aloud, as this will help them to identify where the sentences stop.

STEP 4
Comprehension and consolidation
15 mins

Book reading (5 mins)

- Reread Book 3: A Fine Life.
- Revisiting the book helps to reinforce familiarity with the text and supports phonetic recognition and comprehension.
- For students who need assistance, pair them with a peer or an adult to support their reading

Comprehension (5 mins)

- Ask students to complete **Make a page for a comic** (Activities, page 55).
- Distribute the activity to each student.
- Explain that the comic provided has illustrations missing.
- Ask the students to read the text and draw a picture to match the text in each box.

Extension activities

1 Find the untruths

- Check students have understood the story by instructing them to complete **Find the untruths** (Activities, page 57).
- In this activity, the students are provided with a passage with four untruths in it.
- Ask the students to read the text carefully and underline the falsehoods planted in the story.

2 4-in-a-row game

- Divide the class into pairs and give each pair a copy of the **4-in-a-row game** (Activities, page 63).
- Play with two sets of colored counters. The two players take turns to read the word and put a counter on the word.
- Players can make 4-in-a-row horizontally, vertically and diagonally. The winner is the first to get four of their counters in a row.
- The winner places a counter on a ball. The game is played until all the balls are covered.

3 Write the story

- Invite students to complete the **Write the story in your own words** activity (Activites, page 61).
- Distribute the activity to each student.
- Encourage students to first retell the story orally before writing it down.

STEP 5
Tracking progress

- Assign the **Timed word reading** (Activities, page 52). Students can repeat this activity to improve their reading speed.
- To ensure students are confident with the new sounds, blending, and segmenting, complete the **Spelling assessment and bookmarks** (Activities, page 64) to make a quick, formative assessment of their progress.
- Ask students to read and then blend each of the words.
- Hide the words and ask students to write them out as you read them, encouraging them to segment each sound.
- Depending on your findings, either revisit some of the activities to reinforce any specific skill gaps, or invite students to complete an additional activity from the Activities book.

Extension activities

1 Stepping stones game

- Play the **Stepping stones game** (Activities, page 62).
- This game is suitable for 1–4 players and requires counters and a die.
- Students place their counters at the start of the stepping stones path. They then take turns rolling the die. They move their counter according to the number rolled.
- Upon landing on a stepping stone, the student reads the word on that stone aloud.
- If a student lands on a stone with a directional arrow, they follow the arrow forward or backward.
- The first student to reach the end of the stepping stones path wins.
- Provide positive feedback and encouragement throughout the game.
- For those needing more support, help them to blend the letter sound or word with assistance.

2 Certificates and progress tracking

- Print the **Reading certificate** (Activities, page 130) for students to take home.
- Ask students to check Book 3 on their **Bookmark** (Activities, page 128)
- Check Book 3 on the **Check sheet** (Activities, page 129).

o–e

STEP 1
Preparation

20 mins

LESSON RESOURCES

Learning goal (2 mins)

- Explain to the students that you will be teaching them to read and spell new words using the spelling 'o–e' for the sound /oe/.
- Introduce the book Dandelion Readers VCe Spellings Book 4: The Note.
- You will be completing some activities from Dandelion Readers VCe Spellings Activities.

Preparation (18 mins)

- Introduce the spelling 'o–e' for the sound /oe/.
- Model the sound correctly and ask students to copy.
- or example, say, "This letter stands for the sound /oe/ as in 'note.'"
- Read this list of words: "note," "home," and "bone." For each, point to the letters as you slowly pronounce them, demonstrating how the 'o' and 'e' work together to form the /oe/ sound. Use your thumb and third finger to visually link these letters.

Word building and blending

- Assign the **Word-building and blending** activity (Activities, page 66).
- Ask the students to cut out the letters along the dotted lines, which split the 'o' and 'e.'
- For example, demonstrate with the word "mole" how to separate 'o' from 'e' and then rearrange them by placing 'e' at the end after the 'l.' Use your fingers to reinforce the connection between letters. Draw a link between the 'o' and the 'e' to remind students that 'o–e' is one spelling that has been split.

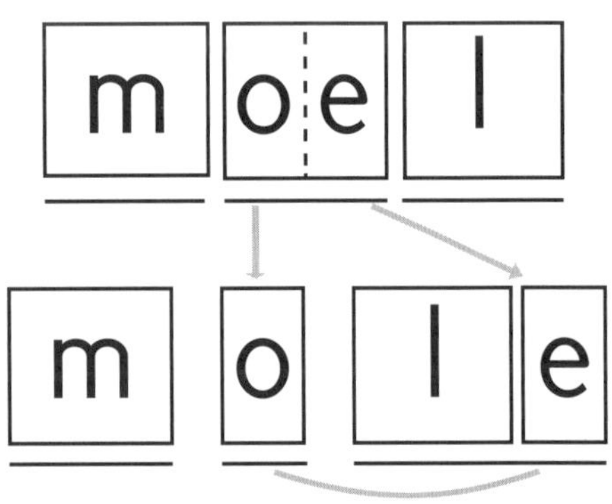

- For the remaining words, direct students through the process of assembling the cut-out letters, always emphasizing how the 'o' and 'e' are connected.
- Explain the spelling rule: even though the letter 'l' separates the vowels, the 'o' and 'e' still work together to form the /oe/ sound.

Extension activities

1 Word reading

- Write the words you have created on the whiteboard (if you haven't done so already). Then ask students to blend and read the words.
- Show how to say each sound individually and then blend them together to read the word. Model blending by using a swishing motion with your finger.
- Encourage students to follow your example with these words: "cone" and "slope."

2 Oral segmenting

- Say a word aloud (e.g. "home") and count the sounds in the word (3). Write the number of lines you need for all the sounds. Now ask students to listen to the sounds in the word and write a letter for every sound in the word as you spell the word.

3 Word chain

- Using sound cards or magnetic letters, demonstrate how to build the word "cone." Explain to the students that you will be making one change to the word. They must be "sound detectives" and notice if you have added a sound, taken away a sound, or swapped a sound.
- Say that you are going to change the word "cone" to "clone." Ask the students to listen carefully to where the change has occurred. Move your finger under the word as you say it slowly. Once the change has been identified, invite a student to swap the sound card or letter. Ask all the students to sound out the word and read the new word, e.g. /c/ /l/ /oe/ /n/ → "clone."
- Direct students through the following word-chain sequence of words: cone—clone—lone—bone—tone—hone—hope—home—hone—cone

STEP 2
Application for reading

15 mins

Before reading (3 mins)

- Revisit the vocabulary taught in Step 1 (e.g. "note"). Clearly say the word: /n/ /oe/ /t/. Explore different definitions for note, such as a written record of ideas or paying attention to something.
- Ask questions such as, "What do you write notes for?"
- Then write the word on the whiteboard and refer back to it throughout the week for reinforcement.

High-frequency words (2 mins)

- Pre-teach or reiterate these high-frequency words: "the," "Toad," "he," "saw," "said," "follow," "to," "onto," "was," "into," "my," "hello," "you," "have," and "me."
- Explain that these are high-frequency words that have tricky spellings the students will learn later. Read each high-frequency word aloud.
- Write the words on the board, showing the separate graphemes in each word. As students learn more of the Alphabetic Code, they will be able to decode those graphemes.

Application (10 mins)

- Once students have started to learn and blend words using the sounds learned in this lesson plan, it's important to provide them with opportunities for them to use their newly acquired skills.
- The chosen text for this reading activity is Book 4: The Note. Briefly introduce the book, its characters, and its context to spark interest and set the stage for engagement.
- Lead students through a directed reading of Book 4: The Note. Encourage students to sound out each word carefully and then blend the sounds together to form the word.
- Provide support by modeling the blending. This hands-on practice is crucial for reinforcing phonetic skills and building fluency.
- Encourage students to sound out each word and then blend to read. This is crucial for reinforcing their learning and for building their confidence.

Extension activities

- Complete the **Fluency** activity (Activities, page 78) to develop students' fluency and prosody skills.
- Create an interactive reading environment by inviting students to take turns reading aloud.

STEP 3
Application for spelling

15 mins

Segmenting and spelling (5 mins)

- Ask students to complete the following activity to practice writing whole words: **Segmenting and spelling** (Activities, page 67).
- In the activity each word is associated with a picture as a visual clue.
- Task students with filling in the squares with the appropriate spelling for each sound.
- Demonstrate correct pencil grip to the class. The pencil should rest comfortably between the thumb and index finger, supported by the middle finger, with the other two fingers curled inwards. The student should have their hands resting on the table and their feet planted squarely on the floor; the paper should be at a slight angle. The student should learn to move the pencil forward using their hand muscles.
- Encourage the students to say the sounds as they write them and then blend the sounds in each word together as they write them.
- After students complete the activity, individually model the formation of each letter that was filled in during the activity on the whiteboard. Focus on the starting point, stroke direction, and completion of each letter.

Sentence dictation (10 mins)

- Read out the **Sentence dictation** sentences (Activities, page 19): "The box had a clock in it! Frank was not late for the next game."
- Encourage the students to sound out the words as they spell them.
- Repeat the sentence if necessary, or read it out in phrases to allow students who may need additional time to process the information.
- For students who finish early or need additional practice with letter formation, you can create your own sentences using the learned sounds and dictate them for the students to spell.

Extension activities

- Ask students to complete the **Punctuation** activity (Activities, page 80).
- Remind students that capital letters are used at the beginning of sentences, and periods are used at the end of sentences.
- Encourage the students to read the passage aloud, as this will help them to identify where the sentences stop.

STEP 4
Comprehension and consolidation
15 mins

Book reading (5 mins)

- Reread Book 4: The Note.
- Revisiting the book helps to reinforce familiarity with the text and supports phonetic recognition and comprehension.
- For students who need assistance, pair them with a peer or an adult to support their reading.

Comprehension (5 mins)

- Ask students to complete **Make a page for a comic** (Activities, page 75).
- Distribute the activity to each student.
- Explain that the comic provided has illustrations missing.
- Ask the students to read the text and draw a picture to match the text in each box.

Extension activities

1. **Find the untruths**
   - Check students have understood the story by instructing them to complete **Find the untruths** (Activities, page 77).
   - In this activity, the students are provided with a passage with four untruths in it.
   - Ask the students to read the text carefully and underline the falsehoods planted in the story.

2. **4-in-a-row game**
   - Divide the class into pairs and give each pair a copy of the **4-in-a-row game** (Activities, page 73).
   - Play with two sets of colored counters. The two players take turns to read the word and put a counter on the word.
   - Players can make 4-in-a-row horizontally, vertically and diagonally. The winner is the first to get four of their counters in a row.
   - The winner places a counter on a ball. The game is played until all the balls are covered.

3. **Write the story**
   - Invite students to complete the **Write the story in your own words** activity (Activites, page 71).
   - Distribute the activity to each student.
   - Encourage students to first retell the story orally before writing it down.

STEP 5
Tracking progress

- Assign the **Timed word reading** (Activities, page 72). Students can repeat this activity to improve their reading speed
- To ensure students are confident with the new sounds, blending, and segmenting, complete the **Spelling assessment and bookmarks** (Activities, page 74) to make a quick, formative assessment of their progress.
- Ask students to read and then blend each of the words.
- Hide the words and ask students to write them out as you read them, encouraging them to segment each sound.
- Depending on your findings, either revisit some of the activities to reinforce any specific skill gaps, or invite students to complete an additional activity from the Activities book.

Extension activities

1. **Stepping stones game**
   - Play the **Stepping stones game** (Activities, page 72).
   - This game is suitable for 1–4 players and requires counters and a die.
   - Students place their counters at the start of the stepping stones path. They then take turns rolling the die. They move their counter according to the number rolled.
   - Upon landing on a stepping stone, the student reads the word on that stone aloud.
   - If a student lands on a stone with a directional arrow, they follow the arrow forward or backward.
   - The first student to reach the end of the stepping stones path wins.
   - Provide positive feedback and encouragement throughout the game.
   - For those needing more support, help them to blend the letter sound or word with assistance.

2. **Certificates and progress tracking**
   - Print the **Reading certificate** (Activities, page 131) for students to take home.
   - Ask students to check Book 4 on their **Bookmark** (Activities, page 128)
   - Check Book 4 on the **Check sheet** (Activities, page 129).

u–e

STEP 1
Preparation 20 mins

Learning goal (2 mins)

- Explain to the students that you will be teaching them to read and spell new words using the spelling ‘u–e’ for the sound /ue/.
- Introduce the book Dandelion Readers VCe Spellings Book 5: Club Rules.
- You will be completing some activities from Dandelion Readers VCe Spellings Activities.

Preparation (18 mins)

- Explain that the spelling ‘u–e’ can make two different sounds: /oo/ (“flute”) and /ue/ (“cute.”)
- Clearly model the /oo/ sound and the /ue/ sound and ask students to copy.
- To demonstrate the /oo/ sound: position your lips as if you are going to whistle, then produce the /oo/ sound.
- To demonstrate the /ue/ sound: position the tip of your tongue just behind your lower front teeth. Keep your lips rounded and slightly protruded. Push air out of your mouth while engaging your vocal cords to produce the /ue/ sound.
- Read the following words: “flute,” “rude,” “rule,” and “cube.”
- For each word, point to the letters as you slowly pronounce them, demonstrating how the ‘u’ and ‘e’ work together to form the sounds /oo/ or /ue/.
- Use your thumb and third finger to visually link these letters.

Word building and blending

- Assign the **Word-building and blending** activity (Activities, page 86).
- Ask the students to cut out the letters along the dotted lines, which split the ‘u’ and ‘e.’
- For example, demonstrate with the word “cube” how to separate ‘u’ from ‘e’ and then rearrange them by placing ‘e’ at the end after the ‘b.’ Use your fingers to reinforce the connection between letters. Draw a link between the ‘u’ and the ‘e’ to remind students that ‘u-e’ is one spelling that has been split.

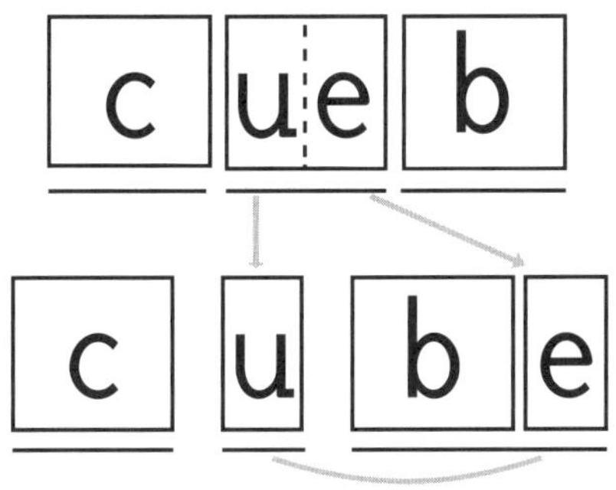

LESSON RESOURCES

- For the remaining words, direct students through the process of assembling the cut-out letters, always emphasizing how the ‘u’ and ‘e’ are connected.

Extension activities

1 Word reading

- Write the words you have created on the whiteboard. Then ask pupils to blend and read the words.
- Show how to say each sound individually and then blend them together to read the word. Model blending by using a swishing motion with your finger.

2 Oral segmenting

- Say a word aloud (e.g. “cute”) and count the sounds in the word (3). Write the number of lines you need for all the sounds. Now ask pupils to listen to the sounds in the word and write a letter for every sound in the word as you spell the word.

3 Word chain

- Using sound cards or magnetic letters, demonstrate how to build the word “mute”. Explain to the pupils that you will be making one change to the word. They must be “sound detectives” and notice if you have added a sound, taken away a sound or swapped a sound.
- Say that you are going to change the word “flute” (moving your finger under the word) to “lute”. Ask the pupils to listen carefully to where the change has occurred. Move your finger under the words as you say it slowly. Once the change has been identified, invite a pupil to swap the sound card or letter. Ask all the pupils to sound out the word and read the new word, e.g. /l/ /ue/ /t/ → “lute”.
- Direct pupils through the following word-chain sequence of words: flute—lute—mute—cute—lute—flute
- Explain that the words in this word chain include both the /oo/ and /ue/ sounds.

STEP 2
Application for reading
15 mins

Before reading (3 mins)

- Revisit the vocabulary taught in Step 1 (e.g. "rule"). Clearly say the word: /r/ /ue/ /l/. Explore different meanings for "rule," such as an instruction for how to behave or a ruler used for measuring objects.
- Ask questions such as, "What rules do you follow in class?"
- Then write the word on the whiteboard and refer back to it throughout the week for reinforcement.

High-frequency words (2 mins)

- Pre-teach or reiterate these high-frequency words: "play," "said," "we," "the," "they," "to," "began," "cheat," "you," "are," "by," "I," and "again."
- Explain that these are high-frequency words that have tricky spellings the students will learn later. Read each high-frequency word aloud.
- Write the words on the board, showing the separate graphemes in each word. As students learn more of the Alphabetic Code, they will be able to decode those graphemes.

Application (10 mins)

- Once students have started to learn and blend words using the sounds learned in this lesson plan, it's important to provide them with opportunities for them to use their newly acquired skills.
- The chosen text for this reading activity is Book 5: Club Rules. Briefly introduce the book, its characters, and its context to spark interest and set the stage for engagement.
- Lead students through a directed reading of Book 5: Club Rules. Encourage students to sound out each word carefully and then blend the sounds together to form the word.
- Provide support by modeling the blending. This hands-on practice is crucial for reinforcing phonetic skills and building fluency.
- Encourage students to sound out each word and then blend to read. This is crucial for reinforcing their learning and for building their confidence.

Extension activities

- Complete the **Fluency** activity (Activities, page 98) to develop students' fluency and prosody skills.
- Create an interactive reading environment by inviting students to take turns reading aloud.

STEP 3
Application for spelling
15 mins

Segmenting and spelling (5 mins)

- Ask students to complete the following activity to practice writing whole words: **Segmenting and spelling** (Activities, page 87).
- In the activity each word is associated with a picture as a visual clue.
- Task students with filling in the squares with the appropriate spelling for each sound.
- Demonstrate correct pencil grip to the class. The pencil should rest comfortably between the thumb and index finger, supported by the middle finger, with the other two fingers curled inwards. The student should have their hands resting on the table and their feet planted squarely on the floor; the paper should be at a slight angle. The student should learn to move the pencil forward using their hand muscles.
- Encourage the students to say the sounds as they write them and then blend the sounds in each word together as they write them.
- After students complete the activity, individually model the formation of each letter that was filled in during the activity on the whiteboard. Focus on the starting point, stroke direction, and completion of each letter.

Sentence dictation (10 mins)

- Read out the **Sentence dictation** sentences (Activities, page 59): "'Rex is rude!' Jill said to Zig and Zog. 'Let's set up a club. Let's not include Rex.' Rex got upset."
- Encourage the students to sound out the words as they spell them.
- Repeat the sentence if necessary, or read it out in phrases to allow students who may need additional time to process the information.
- For students who finish early or need additional practice with letter formation, you can create your own sentences using the learned sounds and dictate them for the students to spell.

Extension activities

- Ask students to complete the **Punctuation** activity (Activities, page 100).
- Remind students that capital letters are used at the beginning of sentences, and periods are used at the end of sentences.
- Encourage the students to read the passage aloud, as this will help them to identify where the sentences stop.

STEP 4
Comprehension and consolidation
15 mins

Book reading (5 mins)

- Reread Book 5: Club Rules.
- Revisiting the book helps to reinforce familiarity with the text and supports phonetic recognition and comprehension.
- For students who need assistance, pair them with a peer or an adult to support their reading.

Comprehension (5 mins)

- Ask students to complete **Make a page for a comic** (Activities, page 95).
- Distribute the activity to each student.
- Explain that the comic provided has illustrations missing.
- Ask the students to read the text and draw a picture to match the text in each box.

Extension activities

1. **Find the untruths**
   - Check students have understood the story by instructing them to complete **Find the untruths** (Activities, page 97).
   - In this activity, the students are provided with a passage with four untruths in it.
   - Ask the students to read the text carefully and underline the falsehoods planted in the story.

2. **4-in-a-row game**
   - Divide the class into pairs and give each pair a copy of the **4-in-a-row game** (Activities, page 93).
   - Play with two sets of colored counters. The two players take turns to read the word and put a counter on the word.
   - Players can make 4-in-a-row horizontally, vertically and diagonally. The winner is the first to get four of their counters in a row.
   - The winner places a counter on a ball. The game is played until all the balls are covered.

3. **Write the story**
   - Invite students to complete the **Write the story in your own words** activity (Activites, page91).
   - Distribute the activity to each student.
   - Encourage students to first retell the story orally before writing it down.

STEP 5
Tracking progress

- Assign the **Timed word reading** (Activities, page 92). Students can repeat this activity to improve their reading speed.
- To ensure students are confident with the new sounds, blending, and segmenting, complete the **Spelling assessment and bookmarks** (Activities, page 94) to make a quick, formative assessment of their progress.
- Ask students to read and then blend each of the words.
- Hide the words and ask students to write them out as you read them, encouraging them to segment each sound.
- Depending on your findings, either revisit some of the activities to reinforce any specific skill gaps, or invite students to complete an additional activity from the Activities book.

Extension activities

1. **Stepping stones game**
   - Play the **Stepping stones game** (Activities, page 92).
   - This game is suitable for 1–4 players and requires counters and a die.
   - Students place their counters at the start of the stepping stones path. They then take turns rolling the die. They move their counter according to the number rolled.
   - Upon landing on a stepping stone, the student reads the word on that stone aloud.
   - If a student lands on a stone with a directional arrow, they follow the arrow forward or backward.
   - The first student to reach the end of the stepping stones path wins.
   - Provide positive feedback and encouragement throughout the game.
   - For those needing more support, help them to blend the letter sound or word with assistance.

2. **Certificates and progress tracking**
   - Print the **Reading certificate** (Activities, page 130) for students to take home.
   - Ask students to check Book 5 on their **Bookmark** (Activities, page 128)
   - Check Book 5 on the **Check sheet** (Activities, page 129).

a–e, e–e, i–e, o–e, and u–e

STEP 1
Preparation

20 mins

LESSON RESOURCES

Learning goal (2 mins)

- Explain to the students that you will be teaching them to read and spell new words using all VCe spellings: a–e, e–e, i–e, o–e, and u–e.
- Introduce the book that the lessons are based around: Dandelion Readers VCe Spellings Book 6: Show Time.
- You will be completing some activities from Dandelion Readers VCe Spellings Activities.

Preparation (18 mins)

1 Word building and blending

- Create words with VCe spellings (e.g. "cake" or "hope") by drawing lines on the whiteboard for each sound in a word.
- Demonstrate how to identify each sound in the word by saying the word slowly and pointing to the letters at the same time. Highlight the split spellings for the sounds /ae/, /ee/, /ie/, /oe/, /oo/, and /ue/. Then sound out all the sounds in the word and move your finger under the word as the sounds are blended, reinforcing the concept of the VCe spelling and how it indicates a long vowel sound.
- Assign the **Word-building and blending** activity (Activities, page 106). Ask the student to cut along the dotted lines and insert the split spellings a–e, e–e, i–e, o–e, u–e into the words.

2 Word reading

- Write the words you have created on the whiteboard (if you haven't done so already). Then ask students to segment, blend, and read the words.
- Show how to say each sound individually and then blend them together to read the word. Model blending by using a swishing motion with your finger.
- Encourage students to follow your example with these words: "wife" and "theme."

3 Oral segmenting

- Say a word out loud (e.g. "tube") and to listen to the sounds in the word. Students then spell the word sound by sound. This is important as it links reading and spelling.

4 Reading and sorting

- Complete the **Reading and sorting: VCe spellings** activity for students to practice differentiating a–e, e–e, i–e, o–e, and u–e words (Activities, page 110).
- Cut the words into reading cards.
- Read each word aloud to the class, emphasizing the correct pronunciation and demonstrating the VCe sound it makes.
- Ask students to sort the words into categories based on the VCe sound they make.
- Students can discuss and compare their choices with their peers to reinforce learning through collaboration.
- For students who need extra practice or finish early, create additional lists of VCe words.
- These additional lists can be used for extra sorting activities to ensure all students are engaged and supported at their individual levels.
- Additionally, the reading cards can be used to play a simple bingo game. For example: draw a card and read the word aloud. Students look for the word on their bingo cards and mark it if they have it. The first student to get three words in a row (horizontally, vertically, or diagonally) shouts "Bingo!" and wins the game.

Extension activities

- Practice blending the list of words on the **Reading practice** page in Book 6: Show Time.
- Play the **Jumping Jack** or **Reading** games in Book 6: Show Time to familiarize students with the vocabulary in the book.
- Use the **Reading practice** cards (Activities, pages 108–109) to play a bingo game.
- Complete the **Splitting two-syllable words** activity (Activities, page 114) to practice syllable division as a strategy for decoding longer words.

STEP 2
Application for reading
15 mins

Before reading (3 mins)

- Revisit the vocabulary taught in Step 1 (e.g. "plane"). Clearly say the word: /p/ /l /ae/ /n/. Explore different meanings for plane, such as an airplane or a flat surface.
- Ask questions such as, "What are planes used for?" Then write the word on the whiteboard and refer back to it throughout the week for reinforcement.
- Explore homophones. Is there another word that sounds the same? Write the word "plain" on the board next to the word "plane". Ask the students, "What is the meaning of the other word 'plain'?" Discuss the difference between the meanings and spellings for the two words.

High-frequency words (2 mins)

- Pre-teach or reiterate these high-frequency words: "show," "said," "the," "robot," "say," "who," "of," "began," "play," "he," "put," "his," "I," "they," "as," "was," "to," "all," "were," and "give."
- Explain that these are high-frequency words that have tricky spellings the students will learn later. Read each high-frequency word aloud.
- Write the words on the board, showing the separate graphemes in each word. As students learn more of the Alphabetic Code, they will be able to decode those graphemes.

Application (10 mins)

- The chosen text for this reading activity is Book 6: Show Time. Briefly introduce the book, its characters, and its context to spark interest and set the stage for engagement.
- Lead students through a directed reading of Book 6: Show Time. Encourage students to sound out each word carefully and then blend the sounds together to form the word.
- Provide support by modeling the blending. This hands-on practice is crucial for reinforcing phonetic skills and building fluency.
- Encourage students to sound out each word and then blend to read. This is crucial for reinforcing their learning and for building their confidence.

Extension activities

- Complete the **Fluency** activity (Activities, page 78) to develop students' fluency and prosody skills.
- Create an interactive reading environment by inviting students to take turns reading aloud.

STEP 3
Application for spelling
15 mins

Segmenting and spelling (5 mins)

- Ask students to complete the following activity to practice writing whole words: **Segmenting and spelling** (Activities, page 107).
- In the activity each word is associated with a picture as a visual clue.
- Task students with filling in the squares with the appropriate spelling for each sound.
- Demonstrate correct pencil grip to the class. The pencil should rest comfortably between the thumb and index finger, supported by the middle finger, with the other two fingers curled inwards. The student should have their hands resting on the table and their feet planted squarely on the floor; the paper should be at a slight angle. The student should learn to move the pencil forward using their hand muscles.
- Encourage the students to say the sounds as they write them and then blend the sounds in each word together as they write them.
- After students complete the activity, individually model the formation of each letter that was filled in during the activity on the whiteboard. Focus on the starting point, stroke direction, and completion of each letter.

Sentence dictation (10 mins)

- Read out the **Sentence dictation** sentences (Activities, page 119): "Pete sat on a throne made of cubes. Jill began to play the flute. "That's a fine tune!" said Pete."
- Encourage the students to sound out the words as they spell them.
- Repeat the sentences if necessary, or read them out in phrases to allow students who may need additional time to process the information.
- For students who finish early or need additional practice with letter formation, you can create your own sentences using the learned sounds and dictate them for the students to spell.

Extension activities

- Ask students to complete the **Punctuation** activity (Activities, page 120).
- Remind students that capital letters are used at the beginning of sentences, and periods are used at the end of sentences.
- Encourage the students to read the passage aloud, as this will help them to identify where the sentences stop.

STEP 4
Comprehension and consolidation

15 mins

Book reading (5 mins)

- Reread Book 6: Show Time.
- Revisiting the book helps to reinforce familiarity with the text and supports phonetic recognition and comprehension.
- For students who need assistance, pair them with a peer or an adult to support their reading.

Comprehension (5 mins)

- Ask students to complete **Make a page for a comic** (Activities, page 115).
- Distribute the activity to each student.
- Explain that the comic provided has illustrations missing.
- Ask the students to read the text and draw a picture to match the text in each box.

Extension activities

1 Find the untruths

- Check students have understood the story by instructing them to complete **Find the untruths** (Activities, page 117).
- In this activity, the students are provided with a passage with four untruths in it.
- Ask the students to read the text carefully and underline the falsehoods planted in the story.

2 4-in-a-row game

- Divide the class into pairs and give each pair a copy of the **4-in-a-row game** (Activities, page 123).
- Play with two sets of colored counters. The two players take turns to read the word and put a counter on the word.
- Players can make 4-in-a-row horizontally, vertically and diagonally. The winner is the first to get four of their counters in a row.
- The winner places a counter on a ball. The game is played until all the balls are covered.

3 Write the story

- Invite students to complete the **Write the story in your own words** activity (Activites, page 121).
- Distribute the activity to each student.
- Encourage students to first retell the story orally before writing it down.

STEP 5
Tracking progress

- Assign the **Timed word reading** (Activities, page 112). Students can repeat this activity to improve their reading speed
- To ensure students are confident with the new sounds, blending, and segmenting, complete the **Spelling assessment and bookmarks** (Activities, page 124) to make a quick, formative assessment of their progress.
- Ask students to read and then blend each of the words.
- Hide the words and ask students to write them out as you read them, encouraging them to segment each sound.
- Depending on your findings, either revisit some of the activities to reinforce any specific skill gaps, or invite students to complete an additional activity from the Activities book.

Extension activities

1 Stepping stones game

- Play the **Stepping stones game** (Activities, page 122).
- This game is suitable for 1–4 players and requires counters and a die.
- Students place their counters at the start of the stepping stones path. They then take turns rolling the die. They move their counter according to the number rolled.
- Upon landing on a stepping stone, the student reads the word on that stone aloud.
- If a student lands on a stone with a directional arrow, they follow the arrow forward or backward.
- The first student to reach the end of the stepping stones path wins.
- Provide positive feedback and encouragement throughout the game.
- For those needing more support, help them to blend the letter sound or word with assistance.

2 Certificates and progress tracking

- Print the **Reading certificate** (Activities, page 131) for students to take home.
- Ask students to check Book 6 on their **Bookmark** (Activities, page 128)
- Check Book 6 on the **Check sheet** (Activities, page 129).

GLOSSARY

Alphabetic Code The framework that shows how the 44 sounds of English are represented by letters and letter combinations.

Alphabetic Principle A fundamental concept in phonics instruction where written letters or graphemes correspond to specific sounds (phonemes) of a spoken language. These sounds come together to form words, which is crucial for learning to read as it allows students to decode written text into spoken language.

Analytic phonics A method of teaching reading that focuses on breaking the word into parts. This begins with an analysis of the whole word, which is broken into onset and rime, e.g. 'fr' + 'og' for "frog."

Blending The process where students learning to read with explicit systematic phonics are encouraged to sound out letters in words and push the sounds together into words. Each letter is sounded out separately and blended from left to right throughout the word. This is the most reliable strategy to read a new word.

Consonant blend Also called a consonant cluster, these are two or more adjacent consonants in a word that spell two or more separate sounds. For example, in the word "stop," the letters 's' and 't' spell the sounds /s/ and /t/.

Consonant digraph When two letters represent a consonant sound. For example, the letters 's' and 'h' spell the sound /sh/ in the word "ship."

Decodable text Text that students can sound out using phonics they have been taught. Decodable texts encourage students to use blending sounds into words as the first strategy when reading.

Decoding Involves translating symbols or letters into sounds and words.

Encoding The process of translating words and sounds into symbols or letters.

Fluency The ability to read text accurately and quickly, including proper expression, known as prosody.

Grapheme A written representation or spelling of a sound (phoneme) in a word.

High-frequency words Common words with "tricky spellings" that students have not yet learned. Students are encouraged to use their phonic knowledge while the teacher provides the "tricky spelling" until the students can decode these words independently.

Letter A character used for representing sounds in speech.

Morpheme A unit of meaning in a word.

Phoneme The smallest unit of sound in a word. For example, the word "cat" has three phonemes: /k/ /a/ /t/.

Phonemic awareness The ability to identify and manipulate individual sounds in words, which includes blending, segmenting, and manipulating sounds.

Phonics A method of teaching reading and writing that focuses on the relationship between sounds (phonemes) and their spellings (graphemes).

Phonological awareness The ability to break down words into smaller parts, such as syllables (e.g. mag-net), alliteration (e.g. Bobby beetle bounced), onset and rime (e.g. m-at), and phonemic awareness (e.g. m-a-t).

Phonology An area of linguistics that deals with speech sound systems and sound patterns of spoken language.

Schwa A weak vowel sound in an unstressed syllable, e.g. the word "chicken" becoming "chickin" or "chick'n."

Science of Reading An evidence-based approach to teaching reading that emphasizes phonemic awareness, phonics, fluency, vocabulary, and comprehension.

Segmenting The ability to separate sounds in words. When spelling, students learn to isolate each sound in the word and represent it with a spelling.

Simple View of Reading A model that demonstrates reading as having two basic components: word recognition and language comprehension. This model offers a clear and effective framework for reading instruction.

Sounds-Write® Reading and Spelling Program A structured literacy program focusing on teaching reading and spelling using a systematic and explicit phonics approach.

Syllables Mouthfuls of words, typically containing a vowel sound.

Synthetic Phonics A method of teaching reading where the reader is taught to sound out individual sounds in a word and blend these sounds together to form the word. This method emphasizes the synthesis (blending) of individual sounds into a word. For example, the word "frog" is learned by sounding out each phoneme, /f/ /r/ /o/ /g/, and then blending these sounds to say "frog."

Systematic Synthetic Phonics (SSP) A method that focuses on the systematic instruction of phonics. In this approach, students are taught to sound out graphemes and blend (synthesize) them into words.

Vowel-Consonant-e (VCe) Spelling When the spelling for the vowel sounds /ae/, /ee/, /ie/, /oe/, /oo/, and /ue/ is split by a consonant. For example, /ae/ is represented as a–e in the word "gate."

Vowel team Two or more letters that represent a vowel sound. For example, the letters 'a' and 'i' spell the sound /ae/ in the word "rain."

Word chain A list of words used to develop phonemic awareness skills such as blending, segmenting, and phoneme manipulation. For example: nip—nap—tap—top—mop—map—sap—sip—tip—nip.

Word A distinct meaningful unit of speech or writing.

3-Cueing vs. Decoding Strategies While the 3-cueing approach focuses on using context and visual cues to identify words, the decoding approach emphasizes systematically breaking down words into their phonetic components. The 3-cueing approach is considered a guessing strategy that can lead the reader away from the text, whereas the decoding approach focuses on letter–sound correspondences in words.